STORM SIGNALS

Other Books by Charles Ritchie

The Siren Years
An Appetite for Life
Diplomatic Passport

Gordon Walked

STORM SIGNALS

More Undiplomatic Diaries, 1962-1971

Charles Ritchie

Charles Ritchie

Macmillan of Canada
A Division of Gage Publishing Limited
Toronto, Canada

Canadian Cataloguing in Publication Data

Ritchie, Charles, 1906-
  Storm signals

Includes index.
ISBN 0-7715-9782-7

1. Ritchie, Charles, 1906-   2. Diplomats—
Canada—Biography.   I. Title.

FC626.R58A37 1983   327.2'092'4   C83-098796-7
F1034.3.R58A37 1983

Macmillan of Canada
A Division of Gage Publishing Limited

Printed in Canada

To my niece Elizabeth Ritchie
and to the memory of
Elizabeth Bowen

Contents

Preface   ix

Washington, 1962–1966   1

London, 1967–1971   85

Diplomatic Attitudes   154

Epilogue   166

Preface

This will be the fourth volume of these undiplomatic diaries. It covers the years 1962 to 1971, beginning with my appointment as Ambassador to Washington and ending when I quit the post of High Commissioner to London and said goodbye to the Foreign Service.

I should from the start warn the reader what not to expect. This is not an historical memoir or a study of the role of Canada in international affairs. Recently a spate of memoirs and studies of this period have appeared. Some are valuable contributions to history—some less so. All were written with the wisdom of hindsight which is denied the diarist.

As a boy I wrote, "I prefer diaries to memoirs. They are less made up afterwards." They are also less flattering to the ego of the author. It is a temptation to revise the record when one comes across opinions about people and events which have since proved to be wrong. That temptation has to be resisted. Also, one does not want to hurt the feelings of the living or cause distress to the friends and relatives of the dead. Yet if one irons out all pungency of comment the sanitized text becomes so bland as to be unreadable. The only real answer to the problem would be for the diarist to die before publication or for those mentioned in the diary to die before him—either seems an extreme solution.

This record is only a footnote to History. Yet History, if not at the centre of the stage, is always in the wings, for the diarist played a small part on the fringes of the drama. Politics dominated the Washington years, and politicians—

good, bad, and indifferent—come and go throughout the story. So too do my diplomatic colleagues. Diplomats are not a particularly popular breed and my old profession, like all professions, has its trivial, sometimes ludicrous, side, but most of its practitioners are hard-headed, humane, and tolerant people who devote much of their energies to the peaceful solution of intractable international problems and the prevention of violent international collisions. As to our own Foreign Service, it contains some of the best brains and most devoted public servants in our country.

Though the framework of this journal is that of the diplomatic career, the diaries themselves are highly personal. The scenes and people appearing in them are an oddly assorted company, not chosen in order of importance or according to the rules of protocol. Why else does the diabolical dachshund Popski usurp space which should be reserved for his betters? Why does the snapshot of an eccentric encountered by accident replace the portrait of a friend whom I saw every day?

In this book statesmen, or would-be statesmen, rub shoulders with authors, society hostesses; old friends re-appear and a younger generation begins to enter on the stage; the scenes shift from Embassy life in London, Washington, and Paris to the streets of Ottawa and the south shore of Nova Scotia. It is a peculiar book because it reflects the changing moods of the writer, ranging from gloom and nostalgia to exhilaration and amusement, written from day to day, sometimes from hour to hour. We diarists are peculiar people; we may appear harmless, yet we can be dangerous. We write things down, awkward things sometimes, indiscreet things, things better forgotten. We should be banned. No doubt we soon will be, for we have no union or lobby to defend us. Diarists are by definition non-joiners; theirs is not a group activity. Our only plea in defence might be that we find Life so interesting that we are not willing to see it slip between our fingers without leaving a trace behind.

Washington

1962-1966

After four years as Permanent Representative to the United Nations I left New York on April 27, 1962, to go as Canadian Ambassador to Washington. My appointment there took place at a time of strained and worsening relationship between the Kennedy administration and the government of Prime Minister Diefenbaker. I had been chosen as Ambassador at the urging of the Secretary of State for External Affairs, Howard Green, and after a prolonged period of indecision on the part of the Prime Minister as to the best candidate for the job. I hardly knew Mr. Diefenbaker personally, and my interview with him prior to my appointment was of the most cursory kind. Howard Green, on the other hand, I knew well. I had worked very closely with him in my capacity as Permanent Representative to the United Nations and I had developed a respect for his ability and integrity, and a personal affection for him. I had serious misgivings myself about my suitability for the Washington post, principally on the grounds that I had not enough knowledge of the trade and economic issues between our two countries. However, the outgoing Ambassador, Arnold Heeney, sought to encourage me in every way possible, and this, combined with Howard Green's confidence, overcame any hesitations I might have had.

To be an ambassador in a capital when relations between your own government and the government to which you are accredited are bad, and getting worse, is always a tricky situation and is a difficult hand to play. I had spent happy years in my youth as Third Secretary in the (then) Canadian Legation in Washington. I had many friends there.

So my wife Sylvia and I were warmly welcomed, and there was not the faintest reflection, in the hospitality with which we were greeted, of the clouds on the political horizon. However, pleasant as this was, it had little to do with the realities of politics. I had only been in Washington a very short time before this was brought home to me. The occasion was a private party at which the Secretary of State, Dean Rusk, was present. To my surprise, he took the occasion to launch an attack on the policies and attitude of the Canadian government in such forthright language that Walter Lippmann, who was among the guests, said to me afterwards that in all his experience he had never heard such terms used to an ambassador about his government. There could be no doubt in my mind, or in anyone else's, of the personal quality of the President's dislike of Mr. Diefenbaker, whom he regarded with supercilious aversion and whose policies seemed to him to have an anti-American bias. Nor could there be any doubt that the Prime Minister reciprocated these sentiments. In Mr. Diefenbaker's case there was anger and irritation, particularly with the President's somewhat arrogant and offhand style. More profound was Mr. Diefenbaker's suspicion, which deepened into conviction, that the President was in close sympathy with the Canadian Leader of the Opposition, Lester B. Pearson, and would not hesitate to interfere in our domestic affairs to bring about a change of government.

For an embassy to be in disfavour with the White House at a time when the office of President was at the height of its power and influence was a disconcerting experience. The word had swiftly percolated down into every department of the United States Administration. As an example, I recall that when, while discussing a minor tariff item, I expressed a differing view from that of the American official involved, he replied that he had the authority of the President for his interpretation and asked me whether I "intended to call the President of the United States a liar."

Despite these strains and stresses, my personal relationship with the State Department and White House officials remained cordial, even friendly. They seemed to regard me more in sorrow than in anger, and their attitude implied—and sometimes more than implied—that I could not, as a reasonable man, be at heart in sympathy with the policies of the Diefenbaker government. While this eased personal relations, it was sometimes more difficult to deal with than outright hostility.

With the Secretary of State, despite his initial outburst, I was on good terms. I respected him as a devoted public servant who had his own difficulties with the White House, and I admired the clarity and precision with which he could outline a case. I enjoyed the earthy sense of humour which underlay his Buddha-like exterior. He struck me as a first-rate executant, rather than an originator, of policy. As he was to demonstrate later during the Vietnam war, he, like many Washington officials, was totally impervious to any idea or suggestion which did not originate in Washington. The United States version of consultation with their allies meant listening patiently to their views and then informing them of American decisions.

McGeorge Bundy* at the White House was always available to me, and at times of crisis I would see him two or three times a week. It was a delight to encounter that steely intelligence, that far-ranging competence, and that sharp wit. He was also invaluable as a mirror of the President's moods and methods.

April 28, 1962—Washington
The first day in Washington. Outside the window in the garden the cherry blossoms, pear blossoms, and magnolias are in the perfection of early bloom. A sturdy Italian gardener

---

*At the time Special Assistant to the President for National Security Affairs, he left government in 1966 to become President of the Ford Foundation.

mops his brow in the heat. The overgrown box hedges scent the air. Inside, a cheerful, polite little Spanish maid trots in and out with breakfast trays. The house exudes the confident, quiet charm of a much-loved and admired Beauty. In all this paradise only Popski is vile. He barks edgily among the bird song and an eye has to be kept on him lest he pee on the acres of pale-coloured carpet.

April 29, 1962

Harold Macmillan is here on a visit to President Kennedy. He met with the Commonwealth Representatives this afternoon. He is certainly my favourite Prime Minister. Talking of Russia he said, "I pin my faith on them gradually getting more like other people, more and more wanting the same things, so that over generations the differences between us and them will narrow. Meanwhile, do not yield to them but avoid picking quarrels." I hope that this pragmatic point of view is the right one but I am far from confident. Of the Common Market he said, "If we do not join the Common Market, do you imagine that in twenty years' time there will be any question of the President of the United States going to the trouble, as today, of consulting the Prime Minister of Great Britain about anything? Why should he do so? We should have dwindled into a small, unimportant island. Europe with its tens of millions would go on without us."

Mike and Maryon Pearson at dinner last night. Mike looks in fighting trim. He does not expect to win the coming election but he hopes to reduce the government's majority or to prevent them from getting an absolute majority.

May 7, 1962

This prolonged period of waiting to present my Letters of Credence to the President is beginning to get on my nerves and I am wondering whether this delay is deliberate on the part of the White House. Max Freedman, the Winnipeg journalist,* says that we are in danger of a state of affairs in which American officials groan when they see a Canadian coming. They think from experience that we are going to grouse over one of our grudges. (As they have a grudge a minute from one ally or another, they must be getting hardened to it.) Max looks back to a time when the Americans turned to us for advice, when we discussed common problems, when Dean Acheson† dropped in to this Embassy to compare notes with our Ambassador, Hume Wrong. Now we drop in to protest, and always in the name of Canadian interests, not on the assumption of shared responsibilities. We are reluctant to admit that we are involved with the United States and have adopted an attitude of some detachment which we associate both with independence and with moral rectitude. Of course no one wants us to agree with every American policy, but there should be a dialogue based on common inescapable commitment. By all means let us stand up to them, but let us talk to them rather than protest to them. Look at the British. Ever since Suez they have been diligently cultivating at every level their contacts with the United States. What an absurdity it would be now to claim that Canada is a bridge between the United Kingdom and the United States. We are the odd man out and it is we who have put ourselves in this position, not only by the content of our policy but by the manner of it. Meanwhile this southern spring weather goes on and I wait day after day in this silent and beautiful house with its cool vistas, mirrored reflections, and blond carpets which muffle sound. From the garden rises the scent of box—strong, sweet, and sexy. It blooms in abandon in what was once a formal rose garden with paved paths and disciplined box hedges; at some time the box got out of control and now luxuriates like a jungle of the

---

*Max Freedman was with the *Winnipeg Free Press.*
†Former United States Secretary of State—statesman and author.

Amazon. There are flowers everywhere and all in bloom at
once—cherry blossoms, magnolia, azalea, wistaria—and in
the Judas tree scarlet cardinals flashing from branch to
branch. All this is too much after the stone-and-steel landscape of New York. My brain feels drugged and drowned in
all this languid sweetness, this trilling of birds and splashing
of water in the goldfish pool.

Popski may feel the same. He has just been sick on the
upstairs carpet from an indigestible meal of magnolia blossoms.

May 26, 1962
I presented my Letters of Credence to President Kennedy.
His reception of me, while perfectly civil, was, I thought,
distinctly cool, and I came away with the impression that this
reflected his attitude towards the Canadian government and
particularly towards Mr. Diefenbaker. He seemed deli-
berately to be creating "a distance". The conversation was
routine and with longish pauses. During one of these the
President half rose from the rocking chair in which he was
sitting, stretched out his arms, and said, "Shoo, shoo." For a
moment I was frozen in my place. The thought passed
through my mind that I might be the first ambassador in
history to be shooed out of the White House. I didn't see that
behind the sofa on which I was sitting, coming through the
French windows out of the garden, was his young daughter,
the little girl Caroline, leading her pet pony. They hastily
backed out of the window into the garden but my reaction
will give some idea of the uncomfortable coolness of the
atmosphere created. What impression did I have of the
President? I had not quite expected the waxy pallor of his
skin. I felt that the man and the image coincided with
uncanny precision, as though he was indeed a TV image
rather than a human being. Even during our strained conversation his calculating, live intelligence was clear, as was the
cutting edge of his will and the jauntiness of his manner.

May 28, 1962

My grandmother, Eliza Almon, was a girl of eighteen in the year 1838 when she wrote her diary, which I have just been reading. Her life was outwardly narrow and funless. She was not an adventurous or pleasure-loving girl and, as she had no eye for character, landscape, or anecdote, her diary is damn dull except in one particular. As to her daily existence, she lived at Rosebank, then a country house on the outskirts of Halifax. The property is now engulfed in streets, though the old stone gates with their rose emblem remain. It was a life of reading, studying French and Italian, sewing, helping with the "housekeeping", going to church twice on Sunday, and walking over to a neighbouring house, Oatlands, on the North West Arm, to see a female friend. Her reading list is wide for a miss in Nova Scotia in those days. It includes Chateaubriand, Byron, Scott, Ford (*The Witch of Edmonton*), Fanny Burney, Disraeli, volumes of French memoirs, and of course Shakespeare, but the real drama of her diary is her spiritual life. Church attendance and good works did not interest her. It was the inner life that absorbed her, and she wrote that she would "more than any temporal evil that could befall me fear being left to the Form of godliness without its life and support." This theme grows in strength and intensity as the journal goes on. It was to be the theme of her life, and she shared this passionately personal religion with her cousin James. When they wrote to each other it was to discuss the sermons they had heard. When she married him she persuaded him to give up the world in the form of a promising career at the Bar and become an unhappy and ill-suited evangelical country clergyman. She died of diphtheria at the age of forty-two, leaving my father and his brother and sisters motherless children. After her death she was always spoken of by the family as a Christian, selfless saint, but my poor grandfather went on fulfilling his duties as a clergyman without heart, enthusiasm, or interest—perhaps without faith?

May 30, 1962

Went to the Cathedral and heard a full and eloquent sermon, but I can't abide sermons, even the best of them. Arnold Heeney, my predecessor here, was a pillar of the Cathedral, which is more, I fear, than I shall ever be. He is a thorough-going Christian of the Anglican persuasion, and his religion, I am sure, guides him steadily in life. During the sermon I kept thinking of the gospel for the day, which included "Knock and it shall be opened unto you". Will it be opened for me? Or don't I knock hard enough? The other day I met a young red-haired Canon of the Cathedral (at any rate, young for a canon) and asked him what was the essential quality for a clergyman, and he won my heart by at once replying "compassion". Then he added, "That is what *I* think; others would tell you 'leadership'."

This is a somnolent Sunday afternoon. Sylvia is asleep in the garden room, Popski asleep in the library, the servants have disappeared to their quarters for a long siesta. Even the birds have gone off the air. It should be a day for reading poetry rather than the prose of T. H. White, author of *The Making of the President, 1960*, a useful, informative book about the workings of American politics. I am filled up to the throat with its gassy, fluent style. It is the story of an American hero by an American hero-worshipper; "There is no ceremony more splendid than the inauguration of an American President", etc. etc. It's all a bit too much to swallow on a hot summer afternoon.

June 2, 1962

Encounter with a leading name-dropper. He began in top form, firing two governors general, the Leader of the Opposition, a French duchess, and John D. Rockefeller across my bows and all but sinking me. Then he began to talk of the Art of Living. I told him that the words meant nothing to me. He admitted modestly that his own understanding of the Art went back to his aristocratic Viennese origins, but he thought I had mastered it, up to a point. "But no," I insisted, "I shall never understand the Art of Living." After three cocktails he rather relaxed and I found myself remembering that I had liked him when we were younger, perhaps before he had so completely mastered the Art of Living.

I walked this morning in Dumbarton Oaks Park by the brown, quick-running stream, then into the close, dark woods of the bird sanctuary and on to the grassy path by the big meadow. Talked at the entrance gate with the gardener, a gnarled, ageless troll. "Been working here for twenty-two years," he told me. "Twenty-seven acres to keep up and not a man or boy to help me." I remember walking in this park in 1939 on the day before I left Washington for my posting to London, and how I came back that morning to the garden of the house in Georgetown and, biting into a peach at breakfast, fancied that I was biting into the fruit of my future in London...how I would write a masterpiece, meet the famous, have a flat of my own and a mistress to go with it. A bright dream—it all came true, except, of course, the masterpiece.

June 5, 1962
Lunched today with Scotty Reston, the Washington correspondent of the *New York Times*. He has been a good friend to me since I came here and is wonderful company. He and Walter Lippmann, and in a different way Henry Brandon,* are a refreshment and a stimulus after diplomatic society. They are also far more important in the political world of Washington than any ambassador. I spoke to Scotty about my unsatisfactory conversation with the President, and by way of consolation he said that in any case the President had not much use for professional diplomats and thinks them a

*Henry Brandon, correspondent for the London *Sunday Times*.

lesser breed of men who are useful if they produce facts or memoranda but do not take the risks or face the decisions of politics. He says that this attitude dates back to the days when the President's father was Ambassador in London, and to the contemptuous view that old Kennedy took of his diplomatic staff.

June 9, 1962
Went to New York to hear Prince Philip make a speech to the Wildlife Fund, which was really an excuse for me to re-visit New York. The city was tricked out in all its best and sending electric impulses of energy into its victims. The women on the streets were as fresh as paint. Girls hipped along the avenue, disdaining the look in the men's eyes. Old painted shrews from Vienna days and matrons from Wisconsin peered into the windows of Bergdorf Goodman. Husky, helmeted workmen, stripped to the waist, lounged over lunch beneath the girders. Inside the monster buildings, middle-aged time-addicts watched for the elevators with hop-eyed intensity and shifted from foot to foot. In Central Park schoolmarms were lining up squads of kids to look at the elephants and watch the seals dive.

June 13, 1962
Dinner the other night with Susan Mary and Jo Alsop.* Seeing Susan Mary brings back memories of all the gaieties of the time in Paris when we first met. I delight in her company and feel that among so many acquaintances she is a friend. Jo is an original, a brilliant journalist and talker, but cantankerous. There is a great cult for him in his circle in Washington. The other day someone said to me, "You must come on Thursday. Jo is coming and is in a very good mood." I felt

---

*Joseph Alsop, author of column "Matter of Fact", syndicated through the *Washington Post* and later the *Los Angeles Times* syndicates, and his wife, Susan Mary, authoress.

inclined to answer, "I'd love to come if *I* am in a good mood."

I had a note today from Freddy Boland, the Irish Representative at the U.N. and an enlivening friend. How much of the friendships made at that time depended on the shared talk of the U.N.? In that U.N. shop there were friendships formed closer than between most diplomats. Those who served together at the U.N. are like soldiers who served together in the trenches—no matter which side we fought on, we know something of the rough-and-tumble of international politics that other gilt-edged ambassadors do not know. When I left, one of my colleagues said, "Don't worry about the workload in Washington. Your problem there will be boredom."

And I am ashamed to say that I *am* bored, and this despite the office responsibilities and the incessant social life. It is something to do with this place, this beautiful bland city, after the high-pressure excitement of New York. This mood has been intensified by reading Durrell's *Mountolive*, which treats of the fate of an ambassador, of the attrition of human ties to which this profession can lead, and of the airless state in which diplomats learn to breathe. Oddly enough, the ambassador in this book has as a companion a pet dachshund who, like Popski, pees on the Embassy carpet.

I suppose if one yawns one's way through a summer day it finally finishes. I can hear the swish of the Spanish maid's broom on the terrace as she sweeps up the dead blossoms fallen from the overspreading acacia tree. The potent smell of box comes in waves from the garden through the still air up to my bedroom window. I have taken off my shirt in this heat and I smell of boxwood as if I were oiled in a bath essence. Damn it, should I take up golf, as the nice New Zealand Ambassador advises? Or hand round the collection plate in the Cathedral with a carnation in my buttonhole? Or shall I end up as that joke figure, a dirty old man?

June 16, 1962

One of the features that emerges from my talks with American officials is their negative attitude towards the Commonwealth. Any reference to its importance in the world falls on deaf ears or elicits an occasional conventionally polite agreement. There are, I think, several reasons for this. The Americans do not like the fact that it includes so many neutralist nations and that it cannot be counted on to support them in an East-West confrontation. There still remains a residual jealousy of it as a hangover of British world leadership. They are now thinking in terms of continental blocs on a global scale, and the Commonwealth cuts across this concept. Or perhaps they simply estimate that it has no future, that its bonds are loosening and will loosen further, that it is a dead duck—or at any rate a dying duck. In terms of Canadian–U.S. relations there may be another consideration at the back of their minds. If the Commonwealth declines or disappears, there will finally be an end to the Canadian balancing act between London and Washington, and we shall inevitably drift further into the American bloc. Certainly London would not raise a finger to prevent this, indeed would view such a development with complete indifference. However, the continued existence of the Commonwealth is important for Canada in other terms—not only because of the advantages of Commonwealth preferences for us but because in its present multiracial form it is partly of our making. We were instrumental in the evolution of Empire into old white Commonwealth, and white Commonwealth into new multiracial Commonwealth. The preference system is perhaps not essential to its continuance but it is an important part of it and a part that is important for Canada. Why should the Americans approve the European Common Market and disapprove of Commonwealth preferences?

June 19, 1962

Henry Brandon of the *Sunday Times* says that the Canadian

government has succeeded in alienating both London and Washington by a mixture of self-righteousness and self-centredness. I think we have got to start looking at developments in the Western world and to try to assess our relationships to them anew. There is no sign of this in the parochial character of our elections. But the United States cannot really be indifferent to the fate of their biggest trading partner and their continental defence partner, so what are their calculations? Are they waiting for us to fall into their laps? Do they discount as mere bluff the anti-Americanism now rampant in Canada and make the calculation that we have got to give in to them in the end, probably hat in hand, and that the rest is posturing?

June 29, 1962
Lunched today with Jim Barco, of the U.S. Mission to the U.N., and the Soviet Ambassador and Madame Dobrynin. Dobrynin skates with skill and ease over the thinnest ice and allows himself a latitude in conversation unlike that of any Soviet ambassador I have ever known. To think that one would live to see the day when Russian and American diplomats gaily joked together about the U-2 incident. Dobrynin is certainly one of the most skilful operators I have encountered in the career. He and I got to know each other when he was in the U.N. Secretariat in New York and are by way of being very friendly. Madame Dobrynin has much smartened up since those days—very cheerful and chatty when she used to be severely silent, and with her hair curled instead of being austerely drawn back from her forehead, her original Soviet-Communist-wife image considerably modified by life in the United States.

June 30, 1962—Evening
Voices and music from a next-door party sounding from behind the screen of heavy-leafed trees bordering the garden. The music plucks at some lost feeling. The women's voices

sound languorous and enticing. It is true, no doubt, that the
encounters between people at that party are as forced as at the
party I have just left, that most are looking beyond each
other's left ear to sight someone more important to talk to.
The laughter in most cases does not contain in its volume one
hundredth part of real laughter and is as tasteless as frozen
ham, but perhaps it is worth coming to a garden setting
under the glassy, unreal light of late evening if two people on
the outskirts of the party remember it as the moment when
they first met, and carry the memory that it was *there* that it
all started.

July 4, 1962
A cool, overcast national holiday on which we are going out
to the country. Tennis for others, and a barbecue. I do not
much enjoy these American days in the country. There is so
much hanging about, and there are so many children and
young-to-middle-aged mothers watching with half an eye
that they don't get into the deep end of the swimming pool.
Besides, no one ever goes for a walk.

Mitchell Sharp has come to see me. He has gone into
politics and just failed by a small minority to beat the
Minister of Finance. He appeared flushed with political
excitement. To see a quiet civil servant so transformed is
astounding—his discovery of himself as a "national figure"
and the inaugurator of new election techniques, etc., is
remarkable. But most of all, at the wave of a wand he has
become a revelation to himself of his own possibilities.
Perhaps I should go into politics!

July 9, 1962
A mixed day. In the morning I went to see George Ball*. He
is one of the most intelligent and attractive figures in the State
Department, but in negotiation, without being unfriendly,

*U.S. Undersecretary of State.

he has shown very little understanding of our position and no disposition to concede anything. In the afternoon, Dick Howland of the Smithsonian Institution came to see me. I was trying to induce him to lend the Hope Diamond from their collection for a Canadian exhibition. We had a very pleasant talk about pictures and people. But he won't part with the Hope Diamond.

July 15, 1962

A neurotic weekend with the servants: the Spanish-speaking maids, with tears filling their large, dark eyes as they tried to explain their devotion to us and their desire to have more time off; Sylvia and the cook, without a common language, stare at each other in dismay and irritation; Colin, the butler, ex-Royal Navy, is a young Scottish martinet, very bossy with the maids, disliked by Sylvia, most meticulous in looking after my clothes, extremely conscious of his status as a butler, which he seems to think gives him dictatorial power over the rest of the staff. Meanwhile, the chauffeur was drunk again last night. I have seen this coming on. If I had spoken to him day before yesterday, when the first signs were visible, I might have stopped him. But as it was disagreeable, I put it off, as I always do put off disagreeable things. And now, I must get rid of him. I suppose if he had not got drunk tonight he would have done it a month or so later. Tonight he drove us right past our house, up the drive into a restricted area at an American military establishment, and stopped the car outside the front door, having apparently mistaken it for our house. I think he has tried to stop drinking but can't. Yet Arnold Heeney kept him on for seven years and never allowed it to come to this. Perhaps it is my fault, in the effect I have on him. I drove the chauffeur in New York nearly out of his mind, and now this chap has taken to the bottle. If he is dismissed at his age, what will happen to him? How can I give him a recommendation, a drunken chauffeur? He's through. Yet he fought in the Dutch Resistance, he's a real man, he's responsible, a professional, never had an accident and probably never will. He has sacrificed his life and career. I might do the same tomorrow, though not for the same reason. How can I judge him? I'll have to discuss it with Harry Stewart at the Embassy and see if something could not be found for him. Damn, damn, damn!

A horde of people are coming to a reception here tomorrow and I am not looking forward to it. It is not that I get bored with other people—it is that I get bored with hearing myself talk to other people.

July 27, 1962

Do the Americans realize that our differences of outlook from them in international affairs make us more valuable to them than if we were mere satellites? I sometimes doubt it. For example, in nuclear matters we are dead against continued tests, so they foolishly accuse us of letting down NATO. Yet now in the anti-test Geneva negotiations we have been able, because of our anti-test attitude, to develop a relationship with the neutral nations which we could never have achieved otherwise, and which has been helpful to NATO. If we had, at U.S. urging, pushed anti-communist protests in the Indo-China Commissions too far and broken out of the Commissions, the whole machinery would have collapsed, and that presumably is not what the United States want. They sometimes give the impression that they do not trust us, but in the long run they do. Why otherwise would they want us in the Organization of American States (which I hope we shall not join)? Now there is a new test case in our policy towards Cuba. Our position is perfectly justifiable, but we have not thought through its implications and simply take the line that as the Cubans have not seized our banks, etc., why should we pull American chestnuts out of the fire? This begs the question as to whether there is a dangerous Communist threat in South America. Sometimes we grudgingly admit this as a possibility. Do we consider what has happened in

Cuba as a popular social revolution and not a Russian-inspired Communist take-over? Is our attitude affected by the fact that, like Cuba, we are a neighbour of the United States? It is unthinkable that anything similar to developments in Cuba should occur in Canada, but if it did, should we not regard this as our own business and resent intervention? In general in our dealings with Communist countries we have tended to be against the policies of economic strangulation (even more against military intervention). While we have never spelled out our views, they seemed to amount to the proposition that economic pressure, sanctions, etc., applied to Communist countries, so far from making them more amenable, make them dig their heels in more deeply. Presumably this is the philosophy behind our trade with China. Of course, our economic interests are the concrete reasons for our policy, but in the background is a philosophical difference as to how best to deal with Communist countries, and our position, though obscurely defined, is basically different from that of the United States.

The more I am involved in diplomatic and political affairs, the more I set store on private feelings. I prefer my loved ones to any political allegiance, and hope I always shall. Henry Brandon talks of his friendship with President Kennedy, with whom he is on easy, almost intimate, terms. I listened with interest and a growing sense of my own lack of contact with the President. Apart from the political strain between him and Diefenbaker, perhaps I am myself out of date—Old Hat in the New Frontier. Washington has always been like this. The "In" people make the "Outs" feel even "Out"-er. It is the same in Ottawa.

August 12, 1962—Halifax, N.S.
We have escaped from Washington for a couple of weeks to come down here with Roley* and Bunny and to see my

---

*My brother, Roland Ritchie, Justice of the Supreme Court of Canada, and his wife, Bunny.

mother. Today is overcast and claggy, the same weather they have had here all summer. Never a day without the sound of the foghorn. It is Sunday, after lunch. It is impossible to believe that one will ever come to life again, impossible to picture life except as a yawn. I cannot walk again in the dank park among the firs and hemlocks. I can't go on reading *Vanity Fair* as I am bogged down among Amelia's tender tears and rhapsodies and I will not skip to get back to Becky Sharp. Popski is bored too. We should never have brought him here. He is driving me mad this afternoon. I mean that not in the casual conventional sense—there really are moments when I tremble for my sanity and fear that if he does not stop barking something will crack in my skull and I shall start barking myself. Poor little brute, he is terrified of the steep, slippery staircase in this house. It takes all his courage and resolution to launch himself from the top step, as if it was a precipitous ski slope, and then he slithers and crashes to the bottom.

Roley is lying asleep in a deck-chair on the damp lawn, looking like Sylvia's sketch of himself. Sylvia and Bunny are making cucumber sandwiches because the Misses Odell are coming to tea. They are Cranfordian, genteel spinsters, unpopularly invited by me. My mother has taken to her bed, totally exhausted by her family. My niece Eliza* has simply gone off the air. A dull Sunday afternoon, but not repulsive. As a family we are happy together, glad to be together, enjoying each other's company more than that of other people, though tomorrow we give our first—and last—cocktail party. The matter of the list of guests has given rise to reproach from my mother because we have not invited a certain couple whom the other guests do not know and may consider socially inferior. The argument for not inviting them is that they would not enjoy coming as they would only be

*My niece, Elizabeth Ritchie, daughter of Roley and Bunny, is called Eliza in these diaries to avoid confusion with Elizabeth Bowen.

uncomfortable and incompatible. My mother treats this with scorn, as being nothing but snobbery. I am alone on her side.

August 26, 1962—Washington, D.C.
I have just returned from Ottawa, where I was summoned to attend Dean Rusk's visit. I flew back here with him in his private jet and had a long talk with him on the plane about all outstanding Canadian-American problems. As on previous occasions, when we are alone and he is out of the office, he talked to me very frankly and told me what was worrying him about our relations, dropping the cautious politeness which he used in his presentation to our Ministers. He talked to me as if we were two officials who shared common assumptions, rather than a Foreign Minister and an Ambassador. If I encourage him in this I cannot complain of the bluntness of his language, but I must not give him the impression that I am detaching myself from the position of our government. It is sometimes a fine line to walk.

Is there something sly about Rusk, a demure slyness like an unfrocked Abbé? Yet I respect his ability and enjoy his company.

August 28, 1962
The Department of External Affairs is becoming more and more a branch office of a huge expanding bureaucracy. Our Foreign Service is becoming more and more like other Foreign Services. This is inevitable, but it does not suit me. I loved the old, small, ramshackle Department where eccentricity was tolerated and where everyone was a generalist who flew by the seat of his pants.

The Victorian Gothic of the East Block was the perfect setting for the Department as it was in those days. The building makes no concessions to efficiency and is a standing rebuke to progress. How many of the waking hours of my life I have spent there; how well I know the dark attics with windows at floor level, one of which I shared as a junior with Temp Feaver and Alfred Rive, and later, on my progress upward in the Service, the spacious rooms with their monumental fireplaces, which were reserved for senior officials. How often have I trod those echoing stone-floored corridors and caught the dusty, musty smell that lingers there from the 1870s. How often have I paused, leaning on that ironwork balustrade that looks down on the pit of the entrance hall, trying to pull together my thoughts before an interview with the Minister or the Prime Minister of the day in his office in the corridor beyond. And how often, too, have I paused there again on my way back after the interview, to curse myself for being talked out of the point of policy that I was trying to make.

I thought I knew every inch of the old place, yet the last time I was in Ottawa I made an unfortunate mistake. Hurrying on my way to see Mr. Diefenbaker about the current crisis, I darted into what I mistook for the men's W.C. What was my horror when I heard outside the toilet closet the sound of women's voices! Fortunately, my presence was concealed by the swinging door that screened the closet— screened, but only to knee level. I determined to stay there until the coast was clear, and tucked my trousered legs around the toilet bowl on which I was seated, to avoid identification. The wait seemed interminable. I had had no notion of how much hair-patting, nose-powdering, and lipstick touching-up goes on among females in these places. No sooner would one leave than another arrived; there was no empty interlude. As to the chat among them, it became positively embarrassing when I heard one of the secretaries giving a living imitation of one of my more tiresome colleagues dictating one of his long-winded memoranda. At last I could stand it no longer. I was cramped from the position in which I was seated, and I was apprehensive as to what more I might overhear—perhaps an imitation of myself. So I swung open the partition and walked through them, without looking from left to right lest I should have the awkwardness of recognizing someone whom I might afterwards encounter in a corridor or office. An astounded hush descended on the ladies at my appearance. What they said afterwards I shall thank God I never knew.

August 31, 1962
I rang up Vincent Massey yesterday and said that I wanted to call on his "experience and imagination" in developing our academic and cultural relations with the United States, as I am very conscious that this side of things is being neglected and that being Ambassador to the United States should mean more than just negotiating in the old civil-servant way with government departments. But I have no capacity for launching a project of my own in this domain. Vincent, I thought, sounded a little cool and dry and said, reasonably enough, that he had no ideas "out of the blue" but invited me to stay with him later in the autumn so that we could talk the matter over.

I saw in the National Gallery today a Crucifixion by (I think) Mathias Grünewald. Christ's body on the cross is in a state almost of dissolution; the face and position of the head show a collapse beyond the pale of sustained suffering. This is the mortal body that dies in corruption. It brought me with a shock to understand that Christ's becoming Man meant that he too came to this subhuman stage of collapse, so different is this picture from the noble, consciously suffering figures on the cross in most renderings of the Crucifixion. Also there is in the Gallery a curiosity of a picture—Christ in limbo among the lost souls. One somehow forgets about that period when Christ "descended into Hell".

September 29, 1962
I have just come back from New York. Yesterday I was walking along Fifth Avenue in the air and light of early-October New York, with the women passing in their newly

fashionable bowler hats, and I was on my way to vodka martinis at the Côte Basque with my pocket full of money. The sun shafts lit on a pansy designer's window full of flowers in baroque vases and it looked as gay and artificial as the designer's dream of it. Men whistled in the street, middle-aged women smiled ineffably, construction workers in scarlet- and wasp-coloured helmets squatted together munching midday sandwiches. In the Central Park pool the seals drifted lazily, half under water. No one for the moment was being robbed or raped or thinking of jumping from fourteenth-floor windows. It was benign October in the well-loved, over-praised city.

Oh, how have my contemporaries attained their self-esteem, how have they added, brick on brick, to the stable structure of a personality that can be turned inside out, public and private, and look the same? Oh, to have principles, to have faith, to have grandchildren, to grow up before you grow old.

September 30, 1962
The Canadian government has certainly made it abundantly plain that we are against nuclear arms as one is against sin, and this moral attitude is shared by the most sophisticated (Norman Robertson) and the least so among Canadians. It is exemplified in the figure of Howard Green. It is not only a moral attitude, but also hygienic; the two often go together in Canada. Fall-out is filthy in every sense of the word. This reaction, strong in many parts of the world, is particularly strong at home. It is from this soil that our disarmament policy grows. That policy may not be rational, but it is very Canadian. Don't forget that for most of our history we were protected by the British navy and now we are protected by the United States' nuclear bomb. All this may be peculiar, it may be unjustifiable, it may be irrational, it may be irresponsible—but no political leader of any stamp is prepared to go

to the Canadian people and tell them that they must have nuclear arms or store nuclear arms. This may change with a change of government; if so, gradually. This is a deep policy difference between us and the United States. At any rate, so long as the present government lasts, (a) we will not fill the Bomarc gap; (b) we don't want nuclear arms for the RCAF overseas; (c) we will not store nuclear weapons; (d) we are against the resumption by the United States of nuclear tests. The United States wants all four of these from us. They are exasperated by our attitude, but so far they are holding their hand. It remains to be seen how long they will resist the temptation to bring pressure upon us of a kind that might bring about a change of government.

As it turned out, the diarist did not have long to wait to witness both American exasperation and American pressure. The precipitant was the Cuban missile crisis in October 1962. The Canadian government resented the United States' delay in informing them that the Russians were installing offensive weapons with nuclear warheads in Cuba, all the more so as Canadian forces were an integral part of NORAD, the defence organization of North America. The Prime Minister considered that, at this moment of crisis when the issue of peace and war was at stake, Canadian support had been taken for granted without adequate consultation. The President was involved from day to day, indeed from hour to hour, in the most testing crisis of his career. The handling of the crisis involved speed, accuracy of timing, and secrecy. In view of the reluctance of the Canadian government to be involved in any action likely to be provocative to the U.S.S.R., it is hardly to be wondered at that the Americans did not wish to become embroiled in discussion with us of the daring moves that they were contemplating to meet the Russian threat. Their reluctance to consult no doubt seemed to them justified when Ottawa hesitated to put Canada on a state of alert, only finally doing so on October 24. Even then, further friction arose when the Prime Minister asserted that the President had asked him to declare a state of emergency in Canada when no such state had been proclaimed in the United States itself. The atmosphere of mutual recrimination that followed between Washington and Ottawa made this a difficult time for the Canadian Ambassador. I regarded the subject matter of the dispute and the high degree of security involved as excluding it from my private diaries. At the time, it was my task, and by no means an easy one, to expound our position over nuclear arms and to explain that we could not go along with any decisions of theirs which might risk a nuclear war without the opportunity to make an informed and independent judgement. Our government had its own responsibilities to the people of Canada. This point of view was represented in Cabinet most tenaciously by our Minister of External Affairs, Howard Green, who in addition had staked his international reputation on his opposition in the United Nations to nuclear testing and at home to nuclear arms on our soil. As to the Prime Minister, I doubted whether he had deep conviction on the nuclear issue, and thought him more influenced by his resentment at Canada's being taken for granted by the United States. The split in the Cabinet over the issue resulted in the resignation of the Minister of National Defence, Douglas Harkness, who favoured the acquisition of nuclear weapons by the Canadian armed forces.

In January 1963 General Norstad, the American retiring NATO Commander, visited Ottawa and at a news conference stated that Canada would not be fulfilling its NATO commitments if we did not acquire nuclear warheads. I found it impossible to take seriously the American official explanation that he was speaking not as a U.S. representative but in his former NATO capacity. This was another American turn of the screw to bring down the Conservative government. In that same month Mike Pearson reversed his previous stand and in a public speech advocated the acceptance of nuclear weapons by Canada.

December 16, 1962
Dined last night with Bill and Mary Bundy. Bill is now in the Defense Department* and Mary is the daughter of Dean Acheson, and very much his daughter too. They are New Frontier and so a welcome change from the collection of ex-ambassadors, Republican businessmen with jewelled wives, and outdated hostesses whom I have been seeing lately. Mary says that her parents are "the gazelle and the lion"—Alice beautiful, gentle, retiring; Dean proud, active, and lord of the jungle—but that now in old age their roles are changing. Her mother sits on Democratic committees while her father more and more loves writing, reflection, and pottering in his potting shed.

At the Bundys' were the Winklers of the French Embassy and the Geylins, he a journalist and his wife, Sherry, an auburn-haired romantic beauty. The Winklers are the only diplomats in Washington who seem universally acceptable. They glide unemphatically from coterie to coterie, welcomed and cherished by all, and are leaving shortly, without any excessive regrets, to return to Paris.

Elizabeth [Bowen] is here. I said to her today that the chilly exhilaration of her new book, *The Little Girls*, must spring from revenge. "Oh yes," she said, implying "you don't know the half of it".

Looking about at the people in the room she remarked, "God has not made enough faces to go round."

December 19, 1962
Lunched with Scotty Reston. I like him very much as a friend and an enjoyable companion. Underneath his Americanism is

*At this time, William Bundy was Deputy Assistant Secretary of Defense for International Security Affairs.

a Scottish subsoil very down-to-earth. I also find him invaluable as a barometer of the political temperature in this city. It is not only that he is extraordinarily well informed, but he has a flair not only for news but for the changing moods, psychological as well as political, of this volatile country. He can sniff a shift in the wind quicker than anyone I know. At the moment he talks in terms of the New Frontier pragmatism. Its practitioners like to think of themselves as tough, young, and hard-headed. McNamara is their hero. I admire them, within limits, but mistrust the application of the business computer to international affairs, particularly when it is allied to power and the love of power.

December 22, 1962
When I woke this morning and saw sun on the melting snow I closed my eyes, pulled the eiderdown over my head, and wished that I lived by myself in an isolated autumnal château in France with high walls round it, with books, a fire in the library, the smell of leaf mould in the garden outside. It was last night's dance that did me in. The guests were all old friends, my Washington pals—twenty-five years later—bringing out into society some their daughters and some their granddaughters. Conversation was a ghostly echo of old jokes and flirtations. Some have been friends or lovers of others; now their children dance together into another generation. Standing in the doorway of the ballroom, beside two ex-young men of my former dancing generation, I was overwhelmed with such a sense of strangeness to think that this grey-haired old guy was I, that youthful eyes travelled over me with that total unseeing indifference which one reserves for lampposts. I did not feel sad, only almost dizzy with the impact of time, hit in the solar plexus by it.

But time stood still when I saw the eternal Tony Balásy waltzing, waltzing in the style he learned in Budapest before the First World War. Gentle, sociable, herbivorous Tony, a gentlemanly giraffe, now nearly seventy. He was the friend of my early days in Washington when he was in the Hungarian Legation, then during the war in London. When Hungary entered the war on the Nazi side he had the courage to resign from his country's diplomatic service, and now has some minor job in Washington and lives in bachelor solitude in a hotel here. Is there something spectral about Tony? A phantom is he? with his elongated, fleshless figure and those bony hands that grip one at the elbow as his mild voice murmurs, "'Allo, Charlie old man."

December 27, 1962
If only one could discard the wardrobe of stale thoughts, concepts, habits, desires, fancies—bundle them off to the old-clothes man. Perhaps that is what Heaven is, to be rid of this accumulation.

A completely still, completely colourless day, of a desolating dullness. It reminds me of some day in my childhood, when I stood alone in the melting snow in a mouldering backyard, wondering what on earth to play.

Only the greedy, ill-tempered little birds are alive in the still garden, engaged in competitive pecking at the food which Sylvia has hung in a bird's hors-d'oeuvre tray from a tree. I am like the old man in Byron's *Don Juan*, trying to get through a long day—"at sixty I wait for six". Damn it, I had forgotten that 350 people are coming to this house this very afternoon to swizzle and guzzle, and the cook is preparing prodigies in the kitchen while Colin, the butler, sets up trestle tables and bars and clears the room of obstructive furniture.

I must stop scribbling and work on my notes for tomorrow's meeting with the State Department on the Nassau Agreement.

December 28, 1962
Had lunch with an old State Department friend in the gloom of the Cosmos Club, surrounded by dreadful portraits of dreadful old men. He is mourning the death of his ninety-

nine-year-old mother. (He himself must be nearing seventy.) Apart from intervals of diplomatic travel he has always lived with his mother and her death has shattered him. His friends find it hard not to find something comic in his stricken state of bereavement. His sister has sensibly—or cruelly—insisted on selling the family home, dispersing the old servants. Now he finds himself exiled to a world of clubs and dependent on luncheon invitations from dowagers. He talked to me today of his lucky escapes all his life from emotional entanglements. He has indeed escaped everything—except Mother. But who is to say that in his love for her he hasn't had as full a life as his contemporaries who married, begat, and took chances?

Reading Genet at disturbing intervals. Am I an existentialist without knowing it? He writes that to utter the words "we doctors" (or "we diplomats"!) shows that a man is in bondage, that that "we" is a parasitical creature who sucks his blood. Perhaps this is what one senses in one's friends who have "improved" with age—that in improving they have diminished from fear of freedom.

December 29, 1962

Went to St. John's Church (the old small church opposite the White House)—poinsettias, carols, and comfortable pews. That old tart Mrs. X was sitting in front of us with a black velvet bow affixed to her doubtfully-auburn hair. Episcopalianism is a long way from existentialism. Then Sylvia and I, accompanied by Popski, went for a married walk. How I do love Sylvia. I can see her now through the window, trundling about the garden in her beige coat with the fur collar. I can hear her scraping earth out of a flower pot and the knocking of the trowel against the pot's surface. It is a mild winter day with a spring sky and some failing snow still on the ground. The birds in the garden are bustling. I feel an after-church drowsiness coming over me and could fall, like Alice in Wonderland, down a deep, deep well.

Yes, I did fall asleep and now it is three o'clock on Sunday afternoon, the day and hour of my birth and always the low ebb of the week for me. But I must bestir myself— Susan Mary Alsop and Dick Howland are coming to tea.

Later: It was very pleasant, tea and cinnamon toast before the library fire, and with Dick and Susan Mary a rich and varied diet of Washington gossip—political, social, with the arts thrown in.

Monday, January 21, 1963—Corpus Christi, Texas

This non-stop tour through Texas has addled my wits. I have given the same spiel in every town—"how happy I am to set foot on Texan soil for the first time", "the links between Canada and Texas", how "Canada is big and so is Texas". Well, there is the famous hospitality, the good nature and friendliness of the people which no one but a crustaceous old boor could despise. Then one is always appreciating, going "ooh, aah, how big it is, how beautiful". No one here ever says anything critical about their own town, each rejoices in living in the best community in Texas (or the world!). This perpetual self-praise rises hourly to Heaven, like incense. Texas is another dimension; it is a cult, too, from which no dissent can be tolerated. It has its converts, not all born Texans. The tall clean-cut young man with the cowboy hat and the Texan accent who has been showing us around Dallas is one of these. When I asked him what part of Texas he came from, his accent seemed to change as he replied, with some embarrassment, "As a matter of fact, I come from Prince Edward Island." The most frightening city in Texas is Dallas, which consists of tall office buildings and hotels entirely surrounded by mile upon mile of carparks. In one direction are the segregated homes of the rich, in another the segregated homes of the poor. The heart of the city has been eliminated. There are no side streets, no small shops, and nothing familiar to attach to. All the inhabitants I have encountered have the same absolutely smooth surface of relentless good humour and optimism. Yet I suppose some-one in Dallas must have time to read, to idle, to mope, to be critical and bad-tempered.

This is the Bible belt, grown rich yet clinging to its values. The oil world is of course an international fraternity. These people are as much at home in Saudi Arabia and Iran as they are in Calgary or Dallas. They fly round the world at the drop of a hat, yet they remain closed to all alien ideas, tone deaf to outside influences. They carry the assurance of their own superiority with them wherever they go. And it is a many-sided sense of superiority. They feel superior in health, techniques, hygiene, and morals, and certainly superior in friendliness.

The Texans I have met distrust and despise the follow-ing: the President of the United States, Washington and all its works, New York City and all its inhabitants, the eastern United States in general, foreigners, Catholics, Irish, Mexi-cans, and blacks, and, as a combination of all that they distrust most, the United Nations. I keep trying to steer the conversation away from the fact that I have served in the United Nations, as any discussion of that organization leads straight onto the shoals, and I am not here on a conversion mission.

Yet everywhere we go—kindness, courtesy, warmth of welcome. This courtesy of theirs is not only on the surface; they will take trouble, do things which are tiresome for them and which put out their lives, and then say, with real warmth, "It is *our* pleasure."

January 25, 1963
How strange it is always to be seeing one's country from abroad as I do. One becomes very conscious, perhaps over-conscious, of the showing that Canada makes in the eyes of others. Perhaps one begins to care too much about what

others think. Also, one builds up a sort of ideal Canada in one's own mind which may have increasingly little to do with reality. What depresses me is the thick coating of self-congratulation which covers every Canadian official statement. This eternal boasting to Canadians about their own achievements when heard abroad sounds painfully embarrassing, especially when combined with a sort of Rotarian optimism about the future in which all Canadian politicians of every party indulge. As for the material with which the Department of External Affairs supplies us for dissemination to the press, it is headed straight for the editorial wastepaper basket. Much of it consists of the texts of speeches (frequently out of date) by Canadian Ministers, aimed at their own constituents and with no relation whatever to American interests and concerns.

I am lucky to have Basil Robinson as No. 2 in this Mission. He has a good tough mind and great sensitivity to the currents of politics, which he has learned in a hard school during his service in the Prime Minister's Office. And he has a passion for integrity and fairness. In addition, I feel him to be a friend and an enjoyable companion. But I think he has his own dry, ruthless yardstick of judgement in which sentiment, I believe, plays little part. At any rate, he avoids making me feel that I am a schoolmaster who has neglected to do his homework and is lagging badly behind the cleverer boys in the class, besides being morally somewhat questionable. This is an attitude conveyed by some of the smugger members of our Department. I find it tiresome. Politicians are infuriated by it in their dealings with the Department. Basil and Ross Campbell are the boys to watch. Ross plays things with more dash—tough little bird. I wonder how he'll end up. He is extremely fertile in policy expedients. Basil is used to the winds of politics but, as a good civil servant, he holds onto his hat in a political gale. Ross might throw his hat over the windmill.

In order to make the following entries comprehensible I should recall that on January 25, 1963, the Prime Minister made a statement in the House of Commons in which he made it clear that he did not regard the storage of nuclear weapons on Canadian soil as part of our NATO commitment. At the same time he indicated that his understanding of the Nassau Agreement, reached a month earlier by President Kennedy and Prime Minister Harold Macmillan of Britain, was a justification for a few months' more delay in arming the Canadian weapons system. On January 30 the Department of State in Washington issued a press release challenging the Prime Minister's interpretation of the nuclear negotiations which had been taking place in secret between the Canadian and United States governments. The Prime Minister was infuriated by what he saw, to use his own words, as "an unwarranted intrusion in Canadian affairs". I had been finding the delays, ambiguities, and indecision of the Diefenbaker government on the subject of nuclear weapons on Canadian soil not easy to explain and defend in Washington. But the heavy-handed and overbearing action of the State Department in lecturing the Canadian government in a public press release seemed to me intolerable. While the State Department protested, with some reason, that they had been obliged to put the record straight over the Nassau Agreement, there could be no doubt in my mind that they welcomed this opportunity to injure the government of Mr. Diefenbaker. The State Department press release had been approved by McGeorge Bundy at the White House. Later it was said that the President regarded this as a blunder on Bundy's part and that he had never himself seen the text of the press release. However, knowing Bundy's political sensitivity and closeness to the President, I considered that he never would have approved the press release unless he knew that it echoed his master's voice.

On February 5, 1963, the Diefenbaker government

was defeated in the House of Commons on a non-confidence motion opposing the government's nuclear policy.

Meanwhile, I had been recalled to Ottawa as an indication of the government's displeasure and as a rebuke to the United States. The Prime Minister and Howard Green were anxious to prolong my absence from Washington, perhaps for a period of weeks, as a further indication of their displeasure with the United States government. I took the line in conversation with them that my absence from Washington would not be particularly shattering to the United States government and I was allowed to return to Washington.

February 6, 1963

Just back from Ottawa. The government was defeated last night. I have been living politics for the last week and feel drained and left without a private thought or feeling after the continuous excitement of this crisis. What a substitute politics are for private life, and what an appalling inner emptiness and surrounding stillness must descend on the politician who is finally and irrevocably OUT. The road ahead in Canadian-American relations is sure to be full of slippery paths and perhaps some precipitous drops. It may also mean the end of my tenure of the Washington Embassy as a small by-product of the general confusion and débâcle.

Oh, those hours in the Prime Minister's Office with Mr. Diefenbaker and Howard Green, two old men, old cronies, old scarred soldiers of political battles. It was indeed an education for me. I had arrived in Ottawa in the hope of repairing the damage caused to the relations between our two countries, but I soon realized that the government was not interested in patching things up and hoped to win an election on the issue of United States interference in our affairs.

In Ottawa during this crisis it was twenty-eight degrees below zero, with winds blowing the icy snow round the

corners and buttresses of the Gothic buildings on the Hill.
Hurrying figures, their coat collars turned up, grasping
briefcases, their heads down against the wind, pushed forward to Cabinet conclaves and parliamentary sessions. The
whole scene was shrouded in the falling snow, and further
mists hung over the river and the airport, completing the
effect of isolation from the outer world which I felt so
strongly in Ottawa, the peculiar capital of a peculiar people.
Then to come back to this bland and sunny scene, this
classical architecture, the wide-spanning bridges and broad
perspectives, this illusion of rationalism. Apart from my
opinions as to the issues at stake, my feelings are very tangled.
While I disapprove entirely of the manufactured anti-Americanism of the government, yet deep down I feel satisfaction at
hearing the Canadian government finally lash out at the
omniscience and unconscious arrogance of Washington, and
I am not immune to that fever of irritation with the United
States government which at home could become a national
rage—could, but I do not think it will.

February 10, 1963
Dear Oatsie Leiter, that generous-natured beauty who brings
a breeze of high spirits into this town, wanted me to meet her
friend, a political lady. We met, but it did not work. She
engaged me on the subject of the Common Market, on which
I have just written a long dispatch. The conversation was for
me like a lesson out of school hours. I stopped listening and
looked. Her pink face was eroded by many suns in Swiss
skiing resorts or the winds that blow on yachts in Southamp-
ton Harbour.

February 11, 1963
The government seems to be falling to pieces, leaving the
Prime Minister more and more isolated in his suspicions,
narrow stratagems, and sterile prejudices. How will it all turn

out? Where shall we find ourselves after the election on April 8? And, incidentally, where shall I find myself?

Diana Cooper* is here on a visit and as usual I find myself talking more frankly to her about my dilemma than to anyone, excepting, of course, Sylvia. It gives me a sense of stimulus to feel that that irreverent, irrepressible Beauty is next door. She is withstanding the siege of old age with all flags flying. I said to her that I thought I had got to the stage in life of throwing in my hand, ceasing to seek for adventure, and "settling down". "Don't," she cried immediately, "don't *do* that," fixing me with her fabulous eyes. "I thought you might advise it," I said. "What, me? Never!", said with immense energy. She has been lunching with the President at the White House. He asked her whether she thought that the loss during the First World War of so many gifted young men who had been the circle of her friends had altered and weakened British political life. She said no.

Today we lunched with Mr. and Mrs. Phillips of the Phillips Gallery, my favourite art gallery. As it is small, one can sit down, and, as in no other art gallery in the world, one is allowed to smoke. I am very much drawn to the Phillipses. He is a bald, rather tired millionaire, with a wedge-shaped head. Mrs. Phillips is a painter and a gallery politician. Her face is worn, not by wind and weather but by exposure to masterpieces. The Lippmanns were there. Walter Lippmann, ever since I have been here, has been a wonderful friend to me. In wisdom, experience, and knowledge of the world he is head and shoulders above most journalists and politicians and, of course, ambassadors! Just before lunch there was a startling crack and the bottom fell out of the glass which Sylvia was holding in her hand. Bourbon and assorted fruits gushed onto the exquisite Aubusson carpet.

---

*Lady Diana Cooper—widow of Duff Cooper, British politician; famous beauty and social figure.

February 12, 1963
I am feeling the strain of these last weeks and completely lost
my temper with a political lady next to whom I was sitting at
lunch. She had been described to me as "a perfect darling",
but I found her a perfect pest and was irritated by some
remark she made reflecting on the Canadian government
which normally I would have passed over without notice.
Also, I keep asking myself whether I could have avoided this
crisis if I had foreseen the State Department press release in
my encounters with Mac Bundy. But I do not think this
would have made any difference.

The feeling of happiness that I experience in dreaming
seems a kind of moral or social weightlessness and, with it, a
gaiety, sometimes hilarity, which is, as they say, "out of this
world". This weightlessness is like that shown in ideal
pictures of blessed beings floating in clouds, but it does not
seem, in the case of my dreams, to be a reward for good
works. Dreaming sorrows are morally awakening and
enlarge the sympathies. Last night I dreamed of her, with
both joy and sorrow.

February 16, 1963
I want to arrange a date for lunch with Dobrynin, the Soviet
Ambassador, next week. He and I have lunch every now and
then. He is very pleasant company, a genial six-footer, a
gleam of humour in the glance behind his rimless spectacles.
He is tenacious in argument, shifting his ground but always
returning to the point. Our talk has usually turned on the
German role in NATO. He speaks of the dangers of renascent
German militarism encouraged and supported by the Alliance. I argue that from the Russian point of view Germany in
the NATO framework, contained and supported by nations
who have themselves had experience of the German aggres-
sion, is safer than a revived Germany free of restraints. But I
make no headway. It is the American-German linkage that

he fears. Perhaps he thinks that Canada might be a softening influence on American policy. If so, he is mistaken. Even if we had such an intention, we would not have the influence.

I had at one time thought of leaving my diaries on my death to my niece Eliza, but why burden the girl with these stale leftovers of a life? Better burn the lot. Eliza is the last of us—no more male Ritchies. The good Lord has decided to discontinue the experiment! She is beautiful and intelligent, subject to gloom, to precipitous moods; has not yet found herself, but with a streak of daring; great charm. I love her and she means more and more to me each year. I am also fascinated by the idea of her future, of what the story of her life will be. I know one thing she will never be—a BORE.

February 17, 1963
I had lunch with my new pal, the Greek Ambassador, Matsas. He is an old aesthete, very astute and also a tremendous old gossip. He has written several enormously long plays, one of which he has lent to me to read. He says that in Europe people say frightful things about their dearest friends—and to them—but go on in friendship, while the Americans never say an unkind word and one can only judge their feuds and hatreds by their significant silences when a name is mentioned.

February 18, 1963
Henry Brandon and Nin Ryan here for lunch. Between them they know all the private scandals, inside stories, of Washington politics and society.

I am in the midst of an argument with the Department at home. What a jealous old hippopotamus the Department is, whose service is perfect submission and who never forgets even if she sometimes has to forgive.

Can the Diefenbaker government live on? I can hardly believe so. How much does it count against the government that the press, many—if not most—businessmen, all civil servants and academics are against them? Not perhaps as much as one thinks. Meanwhile, so far as my own reputation is concerned, I have presided over this Embassy during a time of collapse in Canadian-American relations. Some must surely say that I might have done something to prevent the deterioration. My grandfather put an inscription on his second wife's tombstone: "She did what she could." Hardly flattering to the lady. I suppose that might be the verdict on my efforts. If there is to be a change, won't the new government say to themselves, "Let us start with a new man in Washington"? Then what becomes of old Ritchie? Banishment to our mission in Berne? A kind friend said to me the other day, "In this Canadian-American row it's *you* I am sorry for." Well-meant, no doubt, but misplaced. I do not relish being an object of pity.

February 20, 1963

The Breeses here today with their son. They are my oldest friends in this town. Billy I have known since the days when he was in the U.S. Legation (as it then was) in Ottawa. His mother was kind to me when I was a newly arrived Third Secretary in Washington—had me to stay in her house for weeks. Nora is so lovable, warm-hearted, with a quick spontaneous wit all her own. It is a relief from official life to go to their country house, Longview, outside Washington, like a return to a happier, less responsible time in my life. Thank Heaven for the earlier friends made in this city in my youth and who have remained friends—the Ourousoffs, Anne Perin, Cynthia Martin, and a few others. When I am with them, all the competitiveness and one-upmanship that infect Washington seem to fall away.

Lunch with Diana Cooper. She says that it is necessary for a happy marriage that husband and wife should sally forth separately into the world so that each can bring home something fresh "to put into the vase".

February 21, 1963
Another old friend who is staying with us is Alastair Buchan. I first met him when he was a schoolboy at Eton and spending the holidays with his parents at Government House in Ottawa. I was his best man when he married Hope at Oxford during the war. Then he was a young officer in the Canadian Army; now, after a successful career in journalism, he is becoming known as an expert in international studies. I saw a lot of him during the war in London. We used to have those long, uninhibited conversations, the kind of endless, engrossing talk, well-laced with whisky, which one had with friends in those days when one was unguardedly experimenting with ideas and indiscreetly revealing one's own affairs. Now we are both married, sobered (he more than I, as he drinks nothing), and our friendship is in another key. He has both shrewdness and wisdom and is widely informed on what is going on here and in London, and also in Ottawa. He knows Canada and Canadians from the inside as few Englishmen do and he has an instinct for the country, as his father John Buchan* had before him.

The cook has given notice. She could not stand Colin any longer, with his bossy, butlerian ways. Indeed, Sylvia can hardly stand him herself. He despises all womenkind. His only devotion is not to me, but to my clothes, of which he is a stern but loving critic, proudly attached to certain of my suits and shirts, contemptuous of others. Himself a natty dresser, he is insistent that however I may feel inwardly I must make a good outward appearance. A cocky, curly-haired Scottish introvert, he makes few visible friends, but may have his own

---

*John Buchan, Baron Tweedsmuir, the novelist, was Governor General of Canada, 1935-1940.

resources. It is sad about the cook. She was a good cook, too. Who was it—Saki?—who said "She was a good cook as good cooks go, and as good cooks go she went."

February 22, 1963

Dined at Bill and Mary Bundy's, with her parents Dean and Alice Acheson, and Bruce Hutchison. Bruce is a voice of integrity in Canadian journalism. If this sounds pompous, he isn't. If I had to point to a man who represents what I think of as embodying Canadian qualities, it would be Bruce. He makes friends with those in power but never gives an inch in his estimates of them. And he has a salty, quirky side to him. Dean has a bee in his bonnet about the British—that they are a useless lot who have lost their way in the contemporary world. When I first knew him before the war he was a familiar of the British Embassy; in style, in appearance, even in his London-looking clothes, he is the nearest of all Americans to an upper-class Englishman or Anglo-Canadian. Perhaps that is why he feels free to castigate the British as though he were a member of the family, sitting in a London club among his peers. But his attacks will not be seen like that in London. The mixed feelings that the English arouse among those who have too much admired them are of little interest to the English. They want practical results and do not care whether they get them from someone who does not know one school tie from another. I have seen this operating in Canadian terms. Canadian Tories have, or used to have, a devotion to the "British connection". When they went to London, as Diefenbaker did, they were more at odds with the British Establishment than Liberal politicians who have no devotion to "Crown and Altar".

After dinner Dean Acheson attacked the concept of a multi-lateral force and said it was all nonsense. He said what was needed was sixty divisions of Europeans. As to the commander, he could not be either American or French and might well be a Canadian. Dean says he would put all possible pressure on the Germans to provide military forces. The English would be reluctant to join, he thinks, but might do so if they saw the Germans getting in there first. The Europeans should leave no ground role to the United States. Their sixty divisions could exert pressure on the East bloc and would change the whole picture and lead to, if not reunification, at any rate the withdrawal of twenty Communist divisions from East Germany. He puts all his money on the German contribution and says that NATO is at present a machine without a purpose because we have no intelligible German policy. At any rate he says that if the Europeans will not defend themselves, the United States will not continue to do so.

February 24, 1963
Day before yesterday there was a silly flap in the press about my interview with Rusk. Harold Morrison printed a story that Rusk had "refused to pose with me" for a photograph, and this was spread all over the Canadian newspapers. People will say I have an unlucky touch, but I feel an almost light-hearted fatalism about these misadventures.

March 1, 1963
John Watkins is here, retired from the Service and setting off to Europe to live a little in Paris and follow the sun to Marrakesh. He is an ageless creature, with his crinkled face, small almost-black teeth, and the gleam of intelligence and amusement in his sharp glance. I am fond of him, but there is something impersonal and detached about him that would prevent my claiming to be his friend. I stayed with him when he was Ambassador in Moscow. He said to me, "If you want to understand the Russians, come with me to the railway station tonight." We drove down to the station and there on the platform were dozens of recumbent bodies, wrapped,

some of them, in what appeared to be old sacking to keep out the cold, while others stomped up and down, hands in pockets, collars turned up, whistling and talking. Whole families with small children were encamped in corners. "All these people," John said, "have been waiting for their train for twenty-four hours, and they may be waiting for another day and night. They take all this cold and discomfort quite philosophically. They are without impatience, and the passage of time does not affect them. They have a different time sense from us. Russians are always waiting." When he was in Moscow, John knew more Russian artists, musicians, and members of the intelligentsia than anyone else in the diplomatic corps. He is himself by taste and temperament more a member of the intelligentsia than an ambassador, and eschews formality. He is a curious by-product of the Ontario farm where his old aunts still live (or did till recently). Himself an incorrigible bachelor, they seem his only family attachments.

March 2, 1963
I have been reading Blake's poetry all morning and now am off to lunch with George Ball of the State Department. I want to get on a steady even keel with him, but my own government rocks the boat every time. Only a little more than one month before the election. Today I decided not to go to the Gridiron Club dinner in case someone made an unflattering reference to Diefenbaker and created a further incident. This is indicative of the artificially poisoned state of our relations with the United States. Read *The Loved and the Lost* by Morley Callaghan. At last, a novel not "about Canada" but which takes place in Canada and which shows men and women as walking, talking Canadians, and not written by a visiting Englishman or an expatriate Romanian, but by a real live Canadian. It is not the greatest novel in the world but it does bring us into the territory of literature and so adds a dimension to living in Canada. One thing that

makes for thinness in the air at home is just the lack of this dimension. A cityscape remains a private world until it has been put into words. But winter Montreal, thanks to Callaghan, and Halifax, thanks to Hugh MacLennan, are now on the literary map.

March 5, 1963
The world of Carpaccio...What is the meaning of that figure who appears so often in his pictures, of a young man with long blond hair, sometimes as a bowman, sometimes a courtier, sometimes one of a crowd? His back is always turned to us. What is his face? The face of violence? So it must be in the bowman when he looses his arrows at some suffering saint. And why do those whom he faces in these pictures always avert their gaze from him? Or perhaps he is just a stock figure from a drawing book, chosen to illustrate the tensions of back leg muscles and the turn of the neck. It is sad to see Carpaccio, with his curiosity, his joy in faces, forms, animals, and colours, turn into an old bore in his later pictures. His Christs are repulsive from the start—barber's blocks with somewhat wig-like hair parted in the middle and epicene lips showing in a chestnut beard. Yet his figure of Christ dead is quite different—an elongated corpse with a dark, unshaven face of a young man killed in an accident.

March 8, 1963
One more month before the Canadian elections. For the first time since I joined the Service I am toying with the idea of getting out of it. No, I never shall—I am too inured to it, and perhaps softened by the luxuries that go with it. Yet I seem powerless to prevent the multiplying incidents which are worsening relations between Washington and Ottawa.

March 10, 1963
Sylvia is away and I am in the house alone. This is a house of reflections, green in summer and now, in spring, reflections

of cloud moving and light changing. It is a house of many windows. These upstairs rooms are very quiet, just the swish of traffic on Massachusetts Avenue and of branches moving in the slight spring wind. But early in the morning there is the nerve-tapping noise of the woodpecker in the garden, and later Popski begins barking and goes on and on. I wonder if the spring is driving him mad.

To look around and not always see the same things—it's impossible but it would be heavenly to shift the angle of vision.

March 17, 1963—Snee Farm, South Carolina
We are staying here with Tommy Stone and Alix.* Tommy is in tremendous form. He gets and gives so much fun in life. He is more than the Life of the Party (that would be a desolating description of a friend). Like all performers he is moody and can be pugnacious in a cause, as he was during the war when he espoused the Gaullist cause and pressed it on a reluctant Canadian government. This is the plantation house which he lent to Sylvia and me for our honeymoon. It is a very beautiful place and we were very happy here, except that Sylvia took against the Spanish moss which hangs from the live oak trees round the house—but that did not spoil the honeymoon.

Today there was a luncheon party here. A Southern gentleman with a very loud laugh told stories which he himself found uproariously funny. Jack Wheeler-Bennett was at lunch. He is on a visit to this country. He and I talked about Germany. (His book on the Nazi war machine is by far the best thing ever written on the subject.) Today he was describing his visits to Kaiser Wilhelm at Doorn Castle in Holland and his interviews with Goering before the war. He is a fascinating talker, but his slight stammer gave the

*Thomas Stone, Canadian diplomat, Ambassador to Sweden and subsequently to the Netherlands, and his wife, Alix.

opportunity for the anecdotalist to interrupt with another story.

Much as I am enjoying this visit, I do not think that I should have relished plantation life in the Old South. Some of my Johnston forebears had a place called Annandale outside Savannah and were driven out as Loyalists in the American Revolution. They put in claims for compensation to the British Treasury, enumerating their slaves and acres, I suspect much inflated. The Treasury gave them derisory compensation. The British have never been generous with Loyalists when they were liquidating imperial possessions, as the Anglo-Irish know. Too much loyalty can become an expensive bore. Now the name Annandale has survived as a trade name for a paper company in Savannah and the Southern plantation owners who supplanted the Loyalists are ousted by Northerners. *Moral*: Don't be on the losing side. Incidentally, one of the Johnston ladies of Annandale set a record for carrying propriety to the point of imbecility. Her flounced dress caught fire from a lighted candle. She needed help to get out of the dress but alas there was at that moment only a man-servant in the house. Modesty forbade her to call him in lest he see her disrobed. The flounces flared and she died from the effects of the burns.

April 3, 1963

I took Michael and Andrew Ignatieff,* ages fifteen and eleven, to lunch at the Jockey Club. There was no difficulty about conversation, as when any gap threatened we talked about food, in which both of them are passionately and discriminatingly interested. Andrew is an ageless original and a comic. Michael is a young Russian gentleman of the liberal school, with perhaps a touch of the youthful prig. But that

*Sons of George Ignatieff, Canadian diplomat, subsequently Provost of Trinity College, University of Toronto, and now Chancellor of the University of Toronto.

will wear off, and he is intelligent, interested in everything, articulate—his father's son. But the observant young are on our heels and can't help noticing our vanities and absurdities.

April 8, 1963
Election day. Everyone seems to feel that this is no ordinary election. For some of my fellow civil servants the Liberals seem a sort of normalcy which is called stable government and seems to mean a return to the old middle-class, middle-of-the-way, reasonable, responsible, familiar Canada. But in the process of the election campaign, what is happening to the good name of Canada and the unity of the country? Have we begun to destroy this, and how long is the destruction to continue?

Princess Hohenlohe explained to me at lunch that there was one word of which she did not know the meaning, and that one word was "fear". So fond was she of animals and so confident in their understanding of her love for them that she believed that she could easily walk into a lion's cage, if necessary. I explained that I thoroughly understood the meaning of the word "fear" unless temporarily distracted by interest or desire. The Admiral and a senior State Department official listened to this exchange in silence.

April 13, 1963
In the morning in this house there is a concert of smokers' coughs, Sylvia and I and Colin the butler. Colin was attacked in the street the other day by a man who was attempting to steal his money. He says he threw himself on his back on the pavement and kicked out at the man's stomach. His technique was successful, and the man fled. A woman we know slightly was raped in Rock Creek Park just outside our house at 9:30 in the morning. Instead of concealing the fact, with great pluck she went straight to the police, gave her name and all the details, and said they were welcome to publish them if it led to the apprehension of the rapist.

April 14, 1963
The government is out. Diefenbaker is gone and Mike is in. The wreckage is strewn all around—Ministers with whom I have been dealing in these past years now are relegated to powerlessness. I must at once write to Howard Green to express my respect for him and my gratitude for his steady support. I shall not be writing to Diefenbaker. I consider his disappearance a deliverance; there should be prayers of thanksgiving in the churches. And these sentiments do not come from a Liberal.

April 23, 1963
The new government has been in office less than a week but already one can register a change of atmosphere. So far as I am concerned, I am dealing with someone familiar. Mike Pearson has already telephoned me three or four times. This change does not mean that everything is going to be simple and straightforward in Canadian-American relations, but at least I understand and share Mike's objectives in international affairs. Of course we are still in the honeymoon period. The danger lies in the political weakness of the government and its need for quick political returns.

April 28, 1963
Just one year today since we came to Washington, so Colin tells me. He seems to have a phenomenal memory for past dates and events. Perhaps, like myself, he keeps a diary.

Behind Massachusetts Avenue, if you take a turning up to the left, are the houses of the well-to-do, pink brick in the shade of their trees. Up and down, the well-heeled streets wander into Crescents and Places, peaceful in the sunny morning. On the sidewalk four delivery men stand gazing at a new desk to be moved through a too-narrow gate. A red-headed boy is now jumping from foot to foot, to land on alternate squares in the pavement. Alternations of tree shade and sunlight as you approach the escarpment of flats, and then, downhill, into the rawer sunlight of Connecticut Avenue. Staring through a peep-hole into a waste of shit-coloured mud where the bulldozers nozzle, I see a workman poised on the edge of a crater in the stance of Donatello's *David*. Unexpectedly, I have already arrived at the church. Inside, the dark brownness of cross-beams and high-backed pews, the muffled air at first seeming cool, then stuffy. The eye is drawn to the coloured windows, small and low-set, blue and saffron and the red of throat pastilles. Not a mote is moving in the stillness. Behind closed eyelids the hangover operates—plunging into the subsoil, jetting up into an implausible stratosphere. When the eyes are open they rest on the silent glow of the coloured windows, the rows of dark pews, and the paler vista of the aisle.

May 4, 1963

I am going to Hyannisport with Mike for the meeting between him and the President, and tomorrow I leave for Ottawa for a week's consultations with the government.

May 10, 1963

Back from Hyannisport. The meeting between the President and Mike was tinged with euphoria. The atmosphere was that of clearing skies after a storm—the clouds of suspicion covering Canada–U.S. relations had parted, the sunshine of friendship shone. There was also an undercurrent of complicity between them, as though they had both escaped—like schoolboys on a holiday—from under the shadow of an insupportably tiresome and irrational Third Party and were now free, within limits, to crack jokes at the expense of the Absent One. Indeed, it was mutual relief at the departure of Mr. Diefenbaker from power which gave added savour to the encounter between them. The President and the Prime Minister have much in common—at any rate on the surface, for their natures are different; Kennedy is more ruthless. As companions they are congenial—perhaps the Irish touch in both. They enjoy the same style of humour. More important, they talk the same political language. Their views on international affairs are not widely different, allowing for the permanent difference between the world view of a Great Power and that of a Middle Power. On Canadian-American issues both share the will to achieve solutions to problems in a cool climate without the inflamed rhetoric of the last years. The working sessions at Hyannisport were brisk and business-like. The log-jam of pending issues was broken. It became possible to make progress on a whole range of questions from balance of trade and the Columbia River to air-route agreements for trans-border flights. We have made a new start; it remains to be seen whether the sweetness and light last.

For my own part I made no substantial contribution to this meeting of minds. Mike was more than capable of dealing with the President without advice from me. We had only one long talk the first evening of our visit, when we had a walk by the sea-shore and he outlined some of his preoccupations about the coming talks. He had come accompanied by a squad of officials from Ottawa to whom he could turn for factual information. Otherwise he played it by himself and, as usual, played it skilfully.

At dinner the talk was lively and far-ranging, settling in the end in a discussion of the future of Germany. Of the distinguished company assembled at Hyannisport I most enjoyed that of Annette Perron, the Prime Minister's indomitable secretary. We had travelled the world together with an earlier Canadian Prime Minister, Mr. St. Laurent, and we had a cheerful reminiscent reunion over several post-dinner drinks.

I was installed in Bobby Kennedy's house in the Kennedy compound and retired to bed in an atmosphere of outdoor sport and Roman Catholic piety, surrounded by pictures of sail-boats and by crucifixes.

July 1, 1963—Washington
Our National Day prompts the question: can our country
survive as an independent, united sovereign state—a reality,
not a fiction? Or must we fall into the embrace of the U.S.A.?
We struggle in the net, make fumbling attempts to find our
way out, but all the time are getting deeper in, in terms both
of our defence and of the control of our economy. Diefenbaker tried, in relations with the U.S., to be a sort of pocket
de Gaulle. It didn't work. We have not the will or the means
to be sufficiently exorbitant.

When I asked an old pal of mine how he kept so
cheerful he said, "I see life through rose-coloured testicles."

The woman next to me at lunch yesterday said of her
son, "He isn't as bright as his father, but he is *so* beautifully
oriented."

"Poetry strips the veil of familiarity from the world and
lays bare the naked and sleeping beauty, which is the spirit of
its forms." Shelley, *A Defence of Poetry*. "The veil of familiarity" . . . sometimes it lifts for a timeless moment as it did for
me this early morning when I came back from my walk in the
park to find the house still sleeping. I entered it like a stranger
and saw all things afresh—walking through the silent rooms
wondering, fingering like a child in a house of mystery. I look
about me to take solitary possession. The only motion in the
shrouded stillness is the light breeze sifting in from the empty
gardens. A cardinal flashes past the window on its way to the
drinking bowl.

Talking of poetry and poets, this book of Doris Moore's
about Byron leaves a trail of questions behind it. She defends
the poet fanatically, but doesn't her record work against him?
How was it that he left behind him such envy, hatred, and
malice among those who knew and survived him, so that for
decades the rows among them raged on? Was he unlucky in
his loves and friendships or did he carry some poison with
him? Men and women were carriers of the Byron infection.

Thirty years after his death his wife, his sister, Caroline Lamb, could not get him out of their systems and re-fought his battles.

The influence of the dead on the living—what an endlessly fascinating subject. I believe that my two uncles, Harry and Charlie, one dead the year I was born, the other hardly known by me and dead when I was a child, have by their legends influenced me more than any living man. There must be a medium to carry the current from the dead to the living, sometimes a living survivor, sometimes the written word. My mother was such a medium. The dead lived through her talk. Even their voices and gestures were in the room with you. These were private ghosts, known only to a few. Byron, by the genius of his personality, greater even than his poetry, has changed countless lives...usually for the worse? But he gave them a role to play and a sense of freedom in playing it, even if most were pinchbeck performers. The Byronic virus lasted more than a hundred years—is it now finally extinct?

July 2, 1963
Blazing heat. Woke up early to the whirring sound of the air conditioner and the conviction of the airlessness in the street outside where no leaf stirred. Heat kept at bay by air conditioners is like pain frozen out by a local anaesthetic—in both cases, you know it's there.

Yesterday the Canadian Club had a reception of three hundred people in this house. There are quite a lot of lonely, homesick Canadians living in this town, many of them government employees who come from small places in Canada and are not having so very much fun in this gracious city and missing their friends and relations at home. We sang "O Canada", standing about on the terrace with the written songsheets in hand. Very few people knew all the verses. Sylvia said it moved her and made her want to cry. It was moving when sung like that by a group of Canadians abroad and in the open air and without music. It sounded less like a national anthem than a Highland lament or a nostalgic French-Canadian song full of pride and yearning, not at all martial. It was a good party. How hot the servants were, and how hard they worked. Colin was in his element, ordering everybody about, and old Isobel, the cook, was cheerful, her wild hair hanging about her in elfin locks.

July 6, 1963

The Americans are intensely irritated by our new Budget,* which is being attacked in violent tones by the press. I lunched today with Bill Armstrong at the Jockey Club. He is a good friend to Canada in the State Department and not at all averse to making it known that in this role he has much uphill work to do. At one point he said that when he was arguing with the other American officials for an understanding of Canada's position over the Budget, they said to him, "What Canadians need in financial questions is a psychoanalyst's couch." But then, to the Americans, the irrationality of their allies and their own rationality is an absolute assumption. To do Armstrong justice, he glimpses this. As for our position on this and on nuclear weapons, I am not far from sharing American bewilderment over our tergiversations. These must be called typically Canadian, the reflection of a divided mind. How else was our country held together in the first place? How else will it be held together in the future? Only some do it more expertly than others. If Canada cannot logically work as an independent, unified nation, we are all the same determined to make it work.

Went down in the afternoon to the State Department to see Bill Tyler, who told us nothing about Kennedy's visit to Europe except that the President had lost his suitcase en route

*The Budget introduced by the Minister of Finance, Walter Gordon, was considered in Washington to be anti-American.

with his father's tortoise-shell shoehorn in it, and had found it again on return to New York.

Perhaps, after nearly five years in the United States, I have quite unconsciously begun to accept American assumptions more than I realize. At any rate, I see their difficulties through their eyes, for to the Americans almost everything, and certainly any development in international affairs, constitutes a "problem" to which there must be a "solution". And what spurs them on is the feeling that there is a Russian boy in the class, perhaps more hard-working, who may come up with that "solution" first. Hence they are incapable of leaving anything alone. Also, any "solution" offered is better than none at all. I cannot see that the United States policies which protected and enriched the Western world are wrong. I think they have a more grown-up understanding of the danger of nuclear war than any other government except the Russians'. I share some of their irritation with the ceaseless needling and ungenerous pettiness of many of their allies who depend upon them and vent on them their own resentment of the fact. I think the Americans are right to be continually alert to the Communist danger from which they saved Europe by the Marshall Plan and by the presence of their forces there. Nor do I think they have been guilty in their relations with Canada. I think they have been patient, considering their power. And yet, *yet*, the more I concede them to be right, the more I am subject to fits of what I think claustrophobia. They are *everywhere*, into *everything*—a wedding in Nepal, a strike in British Guiana, the remotest Greek island, the farthest outport of Donegal, the banks of the Limpopo. All countries' private and domestic affairs are of interest to the Americans; in all do they, in a measure, interfere. Everywhere they carry with them their own sense of their own superiority, their desire to improve, to preserve, to encourage what is deserving, to obliterate what is "feudal", "reactionary", "Communistic"; to advance, with banners flying, The American Way of Life, which of course we all must know is the way of progress and enlightenment for all mankind.

July 8, 1963

Had a letter today from Joe McCulley, who was Headmaster of Pickering College, Newmarket, Ontario, when I was there teaching French in 1931. It made me think of that time which I so much enjoyed, although I was a damn bad teacher, sometimes going to sleep in the middle of one of my own classes. One difficulty was my own very uncertain grasp of the subject I was supposed to be teaching. I could speak and read French but my knowledge of the finer points of French grammar, especially the irregular verbs, was so shaky that I had to mug them up the night before I went to class. There was a boy, Llyn Stephens, who knew them better than I did. He would sometimes interrupt as I was teaching, to correct me. Much later in life he became Counsellor at our Embassy in Bonn when I was there as Ambassador. It was a repeat performance. His knowledge of German was far superior to my own, but he no longer corrected me—at any rate in public.

Pickering was an experimental boarding school, founded originally by Quakers. There were no punishments, no compulsory games, and the minimum of discipline. Surprisingly, the system worked remarkably well. This was largely due to the personality of the Headmaster. Joe was then a blond, handsome six-foot crusader, overflowing with enthusiasm. At the same time he had a glance which missed nothing that went on in the school and from which no adolescent subterfuge was concealed. He ruled by magnetism combined with a domineering instinct for command. It seemed unlikely that I should become a friend of this hearty extrovert, yet friends we were. After the school day was over I would often repair to his study, and over a bottle of rye whisky we would talk together for hours. The dramas, personalities, and intrigues of school life gave us plenty of food for conversation. After the second or third whisky we would launch out into wider fields. He would expound his Rousseau-esque vision of the perfectibility of human, and particularly boys', nature. All that stood between the most recalcitrant or idle boy and his happy and fruitful development was the narrow prejudice or brutal mishandling of his upbringing. In vain I pleaded the influence of heredity, as against environment. In vain I argued that while vice might be curable, stupidity was incorrigible. He swept all such objections before him and sometimes, in the final stages of the evening, would recite to me in sonorous tones Tennyson's *Ulysses*. We parted, warmed not only by whisky but by the glow of friendship. Not all the masters shared my enthusiasm for Joe. Some questioned his scholarly qualifications, others resented his technique in discussion, particularly an irritating phrase of his in argument—"Let me clarify your thinking."

My happiness in those early days at Pickering was in part a happiness of contrast. My own experience in the conventional Canadian boys' schools I had attended was deplorable. I had been a miserable schoolboy, untidy (glasses mended with bits of string), uncoordinated in athletics (the English sergeant-major used to say, "Come and watch Ritchie on the parallel bars. It's as good as Charlie Chaplin any day"). I was a natural bully-ee (if that is the word for the bully's butt). I was always late for classes, so spent hours doing detentions—i.e., writing moral maxims in copper-plate—a social misfit cursed with an English accent from my prep school in England; a garrison-town colonial Nova Scotian among the alien herd of smug Upper Canadians. At Pickering I felt that I was getting my own back on a system which had bruised me. So I had a lot in common with those of the boys at Pickering who had themselves either been expelled from or left under a cloud the schools they had previously attended, to come to the freedom and ease of Pickering. Also, having been unpopular as a boy, I found myself popular as a master. Somewhat adolescent myself for my age—I was twenty-four—I shared the rapid transitions of adolescents from hilarious spirits to inspissated gloom. Mentally grown-up, I was temperamentally adolescent. The boys had a sort of cult for me, treating me as something between a mascot and their own freak, in some cases almost their friend. They sensed that I was not interested in improving or influencing them and that I had none of the schoolmaster's way of measuring them. I sought amusement, incident, personality among them as I would have done among my own contemporaries. In the classroom I rarely had trouble in keeping discipline because I viewed classes as they did, as tiresome routine that had to be got through. I was not an inspiring teacher, but the boys did just about as well in exams in my subject as in any others. With younger boys from the Junior School, whom fortunately I rarely had to teach, I could establish no relationship. They found me incomprehensible and uninteresting. Their jerky restlessness, always clattering, banging, and shouting, made me tired, and I never seemed to have the answers to their incessant questions.

Miss Ancient, or Anan as she was always called, was the school matron. It was through her that I had first heard of Pickering College. She had been first my father's secretary and later my brother's governess. At Pickering her sitting-room was a refuge from schoolrooms and school corridors, and from the permanent company of schoolboys and masters—an undilutedly male world. After my early-morning class I used to join her there for coffee and gossip. She was then, I suppose, in her forties or fifties, tallish, flat-chested, and her sympathetic dark eyes gazed somewhat reproachfully at the world through gleaming pince-nez. She was the soul of sincerity, upright and conscientious in all she attempted; an intelligent woman with something touchingly clumsy about her gestures. "My fingers are all thumbs thith morning," she would say in her thick lisp. She and I became friends in those sessions in her sitting-room. I think of her with affection and with sympathy, for her life as the plain daughter of a penniless clergyman had not been an easy one. She had finally found a haven at Pickering where her devotion to the Headmaster was so total that a word of praise or recognition from him made her day, as his occasional impatience with her fussing ruined it. She took a darkly suspicious view of the masters' wives, particularly any one of them who attracted Joe's favourable attention or failed to give full recognition to her status as school matron. In particular she resented one, a beautiful woman with an opulent figure whom the older boys much lusted after. "I suppose," said Anan, "that she has what they call thex appeal." She spoke as though it were an unpleasant, perhaps contagious, disease. Anan's own duties included charge of the school sick-room. Herself stoical, she had no time for malingerers; one half-aspirin was her maximum cure for all forms of pain, and she had an awkward, impatient touch on the sufferer's pillow.

Almost all the other masters except Joe and myself were married men. I often spent my evenings dining and drinking in their hospitable houses. I made friends among them and in the course of doing so learned to understand the rewards and frustrations of the school-teaching career, and to admire the devotion they brought to it. I got rid of my mistaken preconceived notion that schoolmastering was a secondary kind of occupation—"Those who can, do, those who can't, teach"—and came to see it as being important and engrossing. Yet as I moved into my second year at Pickering I was increasingly restless. The atmosphere of youthfulness, at first stimulating, began to be oppressive. Boys were perpetually barging into my sitting-room and lounging about talking and sprawling. No sooner had I got rid of one lot than there was another knock on my door. I began to get bored with their company. They sensed this and seemed to become more boring. Boredom breeds bores. Then, too, it was more and more apparent to me that the teaching profession, admirable as it might be, was not for me. I lacked the wish to mould or to instruct. I saw myself an old crustacean washed over by successive tides of youth. My practical dilemma was that despite years of expensive education I had no qualifications for any alternative job, and 1931 was a notoriously bad year for the unemployed. My only resort was to return from attempting to educate others to being myself further educated. I applied for a fellowship at Harvard, where I had already spent one year as Commonwealth Fellow on leaving Oxford. There were two fellowships on offer: one to proceed to France to explore the significance of the word "sensibilité" in eighteenth-century French literature, the other to advanced studies in the origins of the First World War. I coveted the first and obtained the second. It was to prove a turning-point, for had I been delving into "sensibilité" in the cafés of Montpellier I should not have been in Boston to take the examination for the Department of External Affairs and ergo I should not now, as an aging Ambassador, be sitting at my desk in Washington wasting the government's time with this excursion into the past when I should be studying the statistics of Canadian lumber exports.

August 5, 1963—Halifax, N.S.
I am here on another brief visit to see my mother, who has been increasingly ill lately. She varies much from day to day. Suddenly today the clouds of melancholia and weakness parted, and she was restored to me as she used to be. It was like something happening in a dream. She had returned to take possession with her full nature of that decrepit old body which an hour before had seemed to belong to an equally decrepit old spirit. I was in the presence of a really fascinating woman. It is sad to know that by tomorrow this former Lilian will have disappeared again into the shadows, but it was

worth coming here to be with her for these few hours. Does her brain suddenly clear? What part does boredom play in her afflictions? These questions may be important for oneself some day, if one lives long enough to be in the same case. The doctor says she "talks between the lines", which is a good description. She talked today of religion. She is of two minds about it. She prays without really believing, a process which I share with her. She said to the Dean, fixing him with those extraordinary eyes which even now have not lost all their power, "Do you *really* believe that Jesus Christ is here in this room with us when you are giving me Communion?" She said the Dean answered that she mustn't worry her mind with such questions. "He couldn't really answer me and I shouldn't have asked him. He has his living to make, like everybody else. Being a clergyman is his occupation. How else, at his age, could he earn his living? Anyway, I dropped the subject and offered him a glass of sherry. He accepted, which showed he was a human being."

She dreams, she says, of the next world, "a cold, immense emptiness in which I wander." "But then," she added brusquely, "I pay no attention to such thoughts. It's all nonsense."

A few hours later when I left her she seemed to have recovered from her gloom, because when I asked her how she felt she said, "Fine. I could knock *you* down."

August 27, 1963
Return to Washington. The private world of the family in Halifax is already beginning to recede. The pain over my mother's tragic state will become calloused over. That last evening in Halifax I spent wandering about the streets in the centre of town, past old houses once the homes of family friends, now run-down, decayed, some divided or replaced by parking lots or office buildings. I paused at street corners, seeking for landmarks and seeing the new city which is springing up on all sides and which will be identical with

every other city in North America. I was composing in my mind a requiem for shabby, memory-laden old Halifax.

Back here I am switched abruptly into the present by the Prime Minister's voice on the telephone. Mike is in one of his querulous moods. He asks my advice, brushes it off as irrelevant, then circles back to it, picks up a point I have made, turns it inside out, and makes something of it. What emerges more clearly every day is that the Hyannisport honeymoon is already over. Things have never been the same between us and the Americans since Walter Gordon's Budget.

August 28, 1963
Sylvia has not yet returned. This big house is empty, apart from the servants, and very empty it feels. It was like a Victorian sentimental engraving today when Popski found his way to my lonely side and licked my nose. It is a long time since I have lived alone and I agree with what other solitaries have told me—that the loneliest moment is the early evening, about six o'clock. Also, there is being in bed alone. On the other hand, I rather like having the morning to myself.

Today I went into the town to watch the civil-rights parade, which is, of course, mainly concerned with civil rights for blacks. Washington seemed a ghost town. The population, thoroughly scared of some outbursts of violence, had almost shuttered themselves in their houses. The only other ambassador who had ventured forth was my Greek colleague, Matsas. He says that the other one hundred and three ambassadors have barricaded themselves in their embassies. He himself seemed as debonair and carefree as usual, and takes a very frivolous view of the colour problem.

August 29, 1963
Farewell frivolity. Abandon dreams of visits to New York. A non-stop stream of official visitors from Ottawa is impend-

ing—Cabinet ministers and their acolytes, senior and less-senior civil servants—and I must plunge into a crash course in interest rates and the levels of North American rivers. What is going on in my own Department? None of my friends there write me about the real state of play. They won't put an indiscreet word to paper, but over the second post-dinner drink it all comes out. What do the young men in the Department think of the Old Boys like myself? What do they think of Norman Robertson? Who will succeed him as Under-Secretary? At one time there was a movement on foot "in certain quarters" to drag me back into the job. It seems to have died away. Mike sometimes implies in his half-joking way that I am not "close enough" to the President—what ambassador is? But on the whole, he seems to like having me here. He appreciates that I am not trying to carve myself a place in the limelight—also he knows that I know what he wants done without his having to spell it out.

Dinner with the Inter-American Bank Board. Best food in town, but when I retire, no bank will invite me to be on its Board and I can't blame them.

In the evening the first diplomatic party of the new season. Do these functions at which the diplomatic corps take in each other's diplomatic washing serve any purpose? Certainly not that of pleasure-giving. Perhaps they reinforce the feeling that "Here we are, all in the same boat,"—as though diplomats were embarked together on a cruise ship in foreign waters, unable to get away from each other, jealously comparing each other's accommodation, the places allotted to them in the dining saloon, and their relative precedence at the captain's table, and united in their insistence on their rights as passengers—on such voyages friendships are formed, usually transient but sometimes long-lasting, confidences are exchanged, alliances are consolidated and dissolve or reform before the voyage is over.

Here in Washington there is a latent sense of grievance

in the diplomatic corps. They complain that they rarely have access to the President—even in some cases to the Secretary of State—that U.S. authorities do not attach enough importance to ambassadorial rank, that the important U.S. Senators rarely accept their invitations to dinner, and when they do, often excuse themselves at the last moment.

Today it was a National Day reception. If the number of sovereign nations increases at the current rate and if all are represented in Washington, there will soon be one of these every day of the year. Now some countries are cheating and in addition to celebrating the day they acquired independence or the birthday of their monarch or the glorious revolution when they got rid of their monarch, they give receptions to memorialize any episode in their histories that takes their fancy—a military victory or a transient coup d'état. Other people's National Days are regarded by the corps as a public nuisance and a public duty. They are taken with deadly seriousness by the newcomers on the international scene, particularly the Africans. Maturer nations view them with fatalism, like a woman's attitude to the monthly curse. We have ourselves been delivered by a stroke of diplomatic skill on the part of my predecessor, Hume Wrong, who convinced Ottawa that, as there is no "Canadian colony" of any number in Washington, it was a waste of money for the Embassy to have a National Day reception. It was clever of Hume, because the other embassies in Washington are in the same position as Canada in having few of their nationals here. Apart from bored State Department officials and a handful of senators and fellow diplomats, most of the other guests at these functions are the members of Washington society who do not rate an invitation to a meal. As someone said to me today, "Perhaps we could fit Mrs. X into our National Day. We must have her inside the embassy." A few ancient dames of this breed still survive from the days when I was first in Washington in the 1930s and they have been eating their way like termites through the free embassy refreshments ever since.

A new form of torture is the National Day reception prolonged into a National Film Showing. Unless one is very nippy at getting through the exit, one is herded into a hall in the embassy, parked on a little gilt chair, and subjected to a film portraying some sanitized version of life in the Host Country. These films feature everything from folk-dancing to dam-building, with a lot of boring scenery thrown in— majestic mountains, broad rivers, and vast plains, the latter populated by herds of wild animals stampeding Hell-for-leather for the nearest water-hole—and making one long to stampede oneself.

August 31, 1963

I lunched today with John Sharpe of our Embassy. I have come to have a great liking for him. He was just developing flu, so had an extra drink or two and talked more freely than usual. He tells me that many of the wives in the Department of External Affairs are complaining about diplomatic life abroad because it "unsettles" the children. Why is everybody so frightened of being unsettled? I think it's the best thing that can happen to a growing boy or girl or, indeed, to their parents. It seems that the young-middle-aged lot want to get back to Canada. They have seen through the illusion of exotic adventure abroad and adopted another illusion, that life in Canada has become "tremendously exciting" and that the country is "on the move". Well, it may be so, but I did not notice it in Halifax.

Bob Farquharson, our Press Attaché, since his stroke is always searching for words. The meaning is in his head but the right speech symbol is mislaid. How distracting that must be, always to be looking for words that one cannot find. It's bad enough looking for things about the house—lost spectacles and lost money.

September 1, 1963
I am putting on a belly. That's what comes of trying to develop a "philosophy of life". Meanwhile, there is the question of my future. I think they may leave me here for eighteen months or so. They won't want to appear to change me so soon after the change of government, as it might look as though they were replacing me because I was a Conservative appointee and this would not look good from the point of view of our Foreign Service. Jules Léger, I hear, may be going to Paris. Heaven help him if he has to have dealings with intractable de Gaulle.

September 2, 1963
I am going to switch from drinking rye whisky to drinking Scotch, as I like the latter less and hope I may drink it more slowly. This resolution has been brought on by a long evening, indeed almost a night, since it lasted until 4 a.m., drinking and talking with Scruff O'Brien, the No. 2 Canadian naval man here and a good friend of mine. A restless, intelligent, adventurous man, very Irish and very Canadian, and I like him.

September 3, 1963
I dined with the Australian Ambassador and Lady Beale. They are about the best company in town. Howard Beale says that someone said to him, "President Kennedy is a bore." This revolutionary statement gave us all food for thought, especially Lady Beale, to whom it was particularly welcome, as the President has certainly "un-charmed" her. On the other hand, Alice Longworth, the oldest of all old White House hands, said to me the other day, "Jack Kennedy is a broth of a boy and I love him." I am amused by Alice Longworth, the doyenne of all Washington hostesses and the daughter of Teddy Roosevelt, but I do not love her. I sat next her the other day at lunch. She looked like a witch, in

her big black shovel hat. She is amusing in a gossipy, bitchy way, but not, I find, very funny or congenial.

The Kennedys are given to inviting groups of philosophers, musicians, actors, and writers to the White House. This is a welcome change but I don't know how deep this Camelot culture goes . . . not very far, I fancy.

September 8, 1963

Our new Minister of External Affairs, Paul Martin, arrived on Sunday evening to stay in the house for two nights. I much enjoyed his visit and his company. He is French enough and Irish enough to like a warm, pleasant social surface, and is good company. He is very serious in his approach to his new job, and is widely read and informed about international affairs. He is very much the inheritor of the Liberal tradition in which he was raised—"progressive" but basically cautious and realistic. The first evening we sat and talked. The next morning we had a breakfast party. Colin was in his full glory, deeply gratified to have a Foreign Minister staying in the house. He produced an enormous breakfast in the English-country-house tradition, with numerous side-dishes over flames. The guests included U.S. Senator Morse, who talked absolutely non-stop throughout breakfast, entirely and exclusively about himself.

September 15, 1963

A new officer, Michael Shenstone, has arrived at the Embassy and came to see me today—quick-witted, quick-moving, highly intelligent, ruffled hair, dark eyes gleaming behind spectacles. What must it be like to be a junior officer with me as an Ambassador? My eyes used to be sharp for the absurdities and pretensions of those under whom I served. No doubt theirs are equally so. I don't mind being thought absurd by my juniors, but I should not relish being thought pretentious. What do I, for my part, expect of the people on

my staff? Obvious things—intelligence and hard work. What
do I chiefly deplore? Long-winded wordiness in speech or on
paper. Also, I am embarrassed by incurable stupidity, especially if combined with a conscientious devotion to duty. It is
difficult to know how to report on such cases when they come
up for promotion; one cannot name any remediable faults,
but one cannot conscientiously recommend advancement.
Then I don't like fluffiness of mind which cannot get to the
naked point. That is not so much stupidity as superficiality,
often accompanied by self-esteem. Or, as Anne-Marie Callimachi used to put it: "He is thinking too much for the
amount of brains he has."

I fear that it is not a liberal education, or any education
at all, to serve under me. In my own young days I was indeed
educated by senior men in the Service. Despite all those years
passed as a student at universities, that was the only effective
education I received—education as fitting one for action as
distinct from acquiring knowledge. Hume Wrong was
Counsellor in Washington when I was first posted here in
1937. I can still see him going through my draft dispatches
with his red pencil, looking up across his desk at me with
something between amusement and despair or leaning back
in his chair stroking the back of his head with a rapid gesture
of controlled exasperation at some muddled sentence or
sloppy thought. (A morsel of praise from him would make
my day, for he was no easy praiser.) Style and content he
would scrutinize with impatient patience. He would annotate
my text in his precise, elegant script, and put a stroke or an
exclamation mark of horror beside some solecism. To accompany him on a visit of official business to the State Department was another kind of education. He would arrive for an
interview with his arguments and the facts marshalled in his
mind in impeccable array, and on his return to the Embassy
he would dictate his account of the meeting—a model of
clarity and verbatim recall—accompanied by his succinct

comments and recommendations. Looking back, I now realize that in those days Hume was an unhappy, frustrated man. For although he had such a realistic grasp of policy questions, he was not able or willing to accommodate himself to politicians. He had fallen into disfavour with his peculiar Prime Minister, William Lyon Mackenzie King. In addition, he could hardly curb his contempt for the intellectual shortcomings of his own Head of Mission. Perhaps he was always better in dealing with those under him than those above him. I not only admired Hume, I came to love him as a friend. His cool perfectionism was only the surface—he was warm in his affection. I still often wish that I could turn to talk to him, to hear his acute and biting comments on personalities and events, and to know that here was one man who had never known the meaning of subterfuge or subservience.

September 22, 1963
When I was a young bachelor in Washington my mantel-piece was piled high with invitations to dinners, luncheon parties, and dances. I attributed this to my social and conversational charms. Now I realize that anyone in trousers serves the purpose in the desperate hunt for a spare man for dinner in this widow-populated city. When an apparently case-hardened bachelor takes it into his head to get married, there is lamentation among the hostesses as they cross his name off their lists: "How could he be so inconsiderate?" Death among the elderly single men is unavoidable, but marriage is unforgivable. Among the remaining bachelors my old friend Sammy Hood* is undoubtedly the pearl of price. Not only is he charming, with looks of infinite distinction, but he loves dining out and gives delightful parties in return. And on top of all this, a diplomat and a

*Viscount Hood, British diplomat and Minister in British Embassy, Washington.

Lord. Sammy is made for Washington. He blossoms here, surrounded by affectionate friends, amused and interested by everything and everyone. He makes one suspect that there is a lot to be said for bachelordom, provided one puts friendship before passion. For in a gossipy small town as Washington is, there is no place for lovers. In this and in many other ways it resembles Ottawa. Indeed, Ottawa might be described (in oyster terms) as Washington on the half-shell.

October 2, 1963
To a concert of chamber music at Dumbarton Oaks. Mrs. Bliss greeted us with regal affability. It's a miracle! She hasn't changed in the twenty-five years since first I crossed her threshold—the same tall, svelte figure and erect carriage, the same eager interest in all things cultural, from modern Brazilian poetry to pre-Colombian art. Heaven knows what her age must now be. Washington hostesses are notoriously ageless—they remain embalmed in their own image till one day they crumble into dust, untouched by decrepitude. Artistic hostesses, intellectual hostesses, social hostesses, political hostesses—reigning deities of the Washington stage! There are still a few survivors of those I knew in my youth— Alice Longworth, terrifyingly sprightly, and dear Virginia Bacon, the best-hearted, most downright of the lot, whose dark old house with its family portraits and long gallery still echoes the politics and gossip of half a century. But where is Mrs. Truxton Beale, whose soirées were so famous? And where Miss Boardman, of simple, unassailable dignity? And musical Mrs. Townsend? And where bustling, worldly Mrs. Leiter? And handsome, clever old Mrs. Winthrop Chanler, who had stepped from the pages of Henry James? Washington still abounds in hospitality and there are plenty of cultivated, decorative ladies who in a variety of styles keep the tradition going. I could name a dozen at this moment. But they lack one attribute of their predecessors—they are not formidable. Those old girls could dish out a magisterial snub

and crush a social or political offender with the raising of an eyebrow. Manners have become milder.

Of course now, as then, there are hostesses and would-be hostesses. To an old Washington hand it is both funny and pathetic to see the struggles of some newly arrived political wife or aspiring ambassadress attempting to surprise with novel entertainment or calculated unconventionality. Old Washington, which has seen so many such ambitions blossom and fade, looks on with a basilisk stare.

October 18, 1963
Lunched today with Allan Dulles.* I have been seeing something of him lately. He is not as impressive intellectually, or in force of personality, as his brother Foster or his redoubtable sister. His mind seems to jump about. When seen in the domestic setting it is difficult to think of him as the ruthless spy-master. This afternoon he was shambling around in his carpet slippers, fussing with his notes for a joint TV show, on the subject of American burial practices, with Jessica Mitford and Adlai Stevenson, a bizarre trio. I very much like Mrs. Dulles—she has such individuality and a touch of the unexpected. The other day when I was paying a visit to my beloved Phillips Gallery I saw Clover Dulles standing in front of that great Renoir of the dancing couples in summer sunshine. Her lips were compressed in a line of disapproval and her brow furrowed in puzzlement. When I came up to join her and made some conventional remark about the exhilarating beauty of the picture, she said, "I can't agree. What is all this fuss about? Why do they look as though they were enjoying themselves so much? I can't see why a lot of sweaty red-faced Frenchmen in straw hats prancing about with stout females is so wonderful. I'm certainly glad I wasn't there myself."

Incidentally, one of the Klees at the Gallery has been

*The former head of the C.I.A..

stolen. These pictures are so small that they could almost have been slipped into the thief's overcoat pocket. How I wish it had been my pocket.

November 28, 1963
"Less than a week ago," we all keep repeating to each other in bewilderment and horror. Yes, it is "less than a week ago" since I was in Boston making a routine speech at some civic affair organized by the Mayor. When I sat down at the end of my speech the Mayor rose to his feet and, instead of the conventional thanks, he said, "I fear that I have some extremely bad news to announce. The President of the United States has been assassinated." Sylvia and I walked out into the sunny Boston streets in a state of shock. People were standing at street corners or walking along the pavements weeping openly, a sight I have never seen before. Now the original shock seems buried under these shoals of tributes and eulogies pouring in from all over the world and the hundreds of shifting TV images of the assassination and its aftermath. What can one find to say? The adventure is over, "brightness falls from the air", that probing mind, that restlessness of spirit, are snapped off as if by a camera shutter. We shall no more see that style of his, varying from gay to grim and then to eloquent, but always with a cutting edge.

Now for the anticlimax—to L. B. Johnson. We have come from the hills to the plains.

Bobby Kennedy remains untamed among the flood of public grief. His silence is significant of a deeper and different kind of grief.

December 29, 1963
Now at the year's end I look back on this last year in Washington and try to sum up my impressions. In the first place, there is the life of the office, the management of the Embassy itself. Once a week I sit at the end of the long table

in the Chancery library, with its panelled walls and Grinling-Gibbon-style carvings, where Sir Herbert Marler used to sit with such ponderous dignity when he was in my place and I was a young man. Down the length of the table are representatives of the various government departments stationed here in Washington, also of the armed forces and the Bank of Canada. The Ambassador is supposed to have overall authority for the multifarious activities of Canadian representatives here. It is an almost impossible task to keep track of so many and such varied specialized activities and to know and assess so many varied personalities. Our own people from the Department of External Affairs I of course know well. I have an extremely able No. 2 in Basil Robinson. The younger men from External Affairs on the staff I see very often and they are a very good lot. I manage to keep up with most of the current work conducted here by other government departments. All the same, a great deal escapes me. There are a multitude of direct department-to-department contacts between Ottawa and Washington between officials who have known each other, very often, for many years, while ambassadors have come and gone. Their contacts are close and informal, by telephone Ottawa-Washington, Washington-Ottawa, or by their frequent visits. The armed forces, of whom there are hundreds stationed here in Washington, have their own close relationship with their American counterparts. The Bank of Canada and the Federal Reserve are in touch daily. Many of their conversations, which affect the whole economy of Canada and thus bear heavily on Canadian-American relations, take place on the telephone. Such conversations are not reported, except in the most general terms and not always then, to the Ambassador. All these direct relationships form a valuable ingredient in Canadian foreign policy. The Ambassador, however, is often hard put to it to obtain full knowledge and understanding of all the activities for which he bears a wide measure of official responsibility.

Then there are the frequent visits by Cabinet Ministers and officials for bilateral meetings with the Americans, and each of these Ministers arrives with his own team of experts fresh from the Ottawa scene and highly conscious of the political power-struggles and intrigues going on at home. Sometimes the Ambassador finds himself occupying a figurehead position in such negotiations. This, for example, was particularly true during this year's negotiation with the Americans over the Interest Equalization Tax, when I watched with silent admiration the superb and sustained diplomatic performance of Louis Rasminsky, the Governor of the Bank of Canada, in convincing the Americans, much against their previous stand, that the interests of the United States would best be served by granting us an exemption from the tax.

What, I wonder, was a diplomat's life like before the invention of the telephone? Ministers and officials, particularly of course officials of my own Department, are on the telephone to me almost daily, and so, quite frequently, is the Prime Minister. None of them seem to pay the slightest attention to the regulations supposed to govern the use of the telephone in the interests of security. Cabinet Ministers are particularly irresponsible in what they say, but then I should think, one way or another, the Americans know virtually everything that goes on in the activities of the Embassy if they are sufficiently interested to find out. Mike has never been particularly careful on this score. The fact that I have known him for so many years, however, makes it easy for me to pick up his meaning and intention from a half-phrase, sometimes even from the tone of his voice. In these recent years since he has been in politics I have been more and more struck by the tenacity with which he pursues his objectives. He does not proceed in a straight line, but crab-wise. If he meets an obstacle, he turns aside, even appearing to forget his intention, but he always comes back to what he was originally seeking. In his conversations with his American counterparts or in the days when, as Foreign Minister, he played such a part in the United Nations, he showed extraordinary facility in devising compromise, in finding a formula, often scribbled on the back of an envelope in the heat of debate. Indeed, his diplomatic footwork is amazingly nimble. One aspect of his character of which one has to beware, and which often leads the unwary into misunderstanding, is his acute dislike of any personal unpleasantness. Thus he often leaves the impression of agreeing to more than he intends to fulfil. People leave him with the impression that he has adopted their views when in fact he is simply trying to save their faces. Indeed, I have found that ready agreement on his part to any proposition is a negative sign. When I worked with him in the Department of External Affairs, I found that if he praised any proposition I put to him, it was speedily put aside. If, on the other hand, he poured forth a stream of objections and appeared to brush the proposal away, it was a sign that he was taking a serious interest in it. From the personal point of view it is, of course, a relief and a stimulus to me to be dealing with a Prime Minister who is also a friend.

My relations with the State Department are also, of course, easier since the change of government, although they never were difficult on a personal basis. Apart from Rusk himself, I see a good deal of Bill Bundy, a very nice and very able man. He and his wife Mary are personal friends. In general, the State Department strike me as highly competent but extremely cautious in the expression of their views. I wonder whether this is a hangover from the McCarthy years and the attacks on the State Department for supposedly left-wing inclinations. American officials are less willing to discuss alternatives, less speculative and less forthcoming, than the Foreign Office in London. They also seem somewhat less individual in their views than our own people at home. They tend to run to a pattern. There are outstanding exceptions.

One is George Ball, a forceful, original mind, very tough in negotiation but very civilized in conversation. (He shares my love and admiration for the novels of Anthony Powell.) Another outstanding exception is Averell Harriman.* That old man is younger in mind and in spirit than many of his juniors, and has more political imagination; multi-millionaire, a former politician, he is totally without pomposity. Of the older men, Dean Acheson, now on the fringe of affairs, is my closest friend. I have known him and his beautiful and perceptive wife, Alice, since my early days in Washington. It stimulates one's mind just to be in the room with him. He has such immense style, intellectual and social. His vanity is endearing. We often go during the weekend for lunch with the Achesons at their country house. He always runs up the Canadian flag when I arrive. He is a kind of Canadian himself by ancestry and in temperament. This makes for difficulties with him, as he feels perfectly free, as if he were himself a Canadian citizen, to launch into the most violent attacks on Canadian policy, and in particular on Mike Pearson, for whom he has conceived strong mistrust. Once at his house after lunch he attacked Mike's reputation in such terms that I thought that as we were talking of my Prime Minister I should perhaps leave the house, after having in vain attempted to contradict him. However, as he then turned to an equally lively attack on most American political figures, I felt that it would be idle and absurd to make a scene and that my admiration and friendship for him were more important than anything he said.

Then as to my dealings with the White House this year, there has been the pleasure and stimulus of working with Mac Bundy. His company gives me the same kind of pleasure as that of Dag Hammarskjöld or Isaiah Berlin—the

*At this time Harriman had just left the post of Assistant Secretary of State for Far Eastern Affairs to become Undersecretary of State for Political Affairs. From 1965 to 1968 he was to serve as Ambassador-at-Large.

quickness of his mind, that network of live intelligence. To some, Mac's intellectual cocksureness might be putting-off, but then they are all cocksure here, all the leading officials—Ball, Acheson, Rusk, McNamara, and so on, right down the line. And at the top, in the Presidency, there is no humility, no self-doubt. The cast of thought in Washington is absolutist. It is true that there are a number of incompatible Absolutists, often in embattled struggle with each other, but all are Absolute for America, this super-nation of theirs which charges through inner and outer space engined by inexhaustible energy, confident in its right direction, the one and only inheritor of all the empires and the one which most fears and condemns the name of Empire, the United States of America, exhorting, protecting, preaching to and profiting by—half the world.

I don't know what I should have done since I came to Washington without my journalist friends. Some of my colleagues mistrust journalists, some are simply scared of them. I have always enjoyed their company. After all, I once tried to be a journalist myself—and failed. In Washington the top journalists wield more influence and have more access to the seats of the mighty than any diplomats. For example, Walter Lippmann. Walter is one of the most interesting minds I have encountered, also one of the most congenial companions. I have lunched with him at regular intervals this year and we go to the gatherings at the Lippmanns' house where one meets some of the inner circle of Washington influence. Then Scotty Reston has proved to be as good a friend to me as he has to other Canadian representatives and to our country.

As to the diplomatic colleagues, I have seen less of them than I used to do at the United Nations, yet we are often in and out of their Embassies and they are often here. David Ormsby-Gore, the British Ambassador, was the closest to President Kennedy of all the diplomats, although I don't know how much British influence affected the major policy decisions taken in the White House. The same question arises about my opposite number, Walt Butterworth, the American Ambassador in Ottawa. Walt is an able and aggressive operator. He has known Mike Pearson since years ago when he was a junior in the American Embassy and Mike was in the Department of External Affairs, and he sees him very often on an intimate social basis. Again, I rather doubt that he influences Mike's political decisions.

Thank God we have many friends in this city who have nothing to do with politics (except that everyone in Washington, directly or indirectly, has something to do with politics). Sylvia likes it here very much. She has a lot of women friends and it is a great place for women's group activities. She knows more Senators' wives than I know Senators. I think she is thoroughly enjoying herself. As for me, what a fortunate day it was when she said she would marry me.

I am lucky in having a lot of old friends here who date back to before the war. Some of these are actual born-and-bred Washingtonians, "the cave-dwellers", who have seen the ups and downs of so many political reputations, the coming and going of so many confidential advisers to successive presidents. Since I came back to Washington this time we have made a lot of new friends. Yet someone remarked to me the other day, "In this town no one is missed when they go away and no one is forgotten when they come back." Yes, Washington is a movable feast. Personally I am not in favour of capitals created purely for political purposes—Washington, Ottawa, Bonn. I think the capital of a nation should be in one of the great cities where the political process is not isolated. There is a claustrophobia about federal capitals.

Well, goodbye 1963. It closes on the note on which it opened—politics, the fascinating, dangerous world on whose fringe I live and whose muddied waters I try to keep my head above.

Here the diaries abruptly end, not to be resumed for nearly four years. What has become of the missing years? The volumes were perhaps lost in subsequent migrations from one diplomatic post to another? Left in the drawer of a hotel bedroom in Paris, London, or New York? Or did they ever exist at all—was I visited by one of those merciful intermissions when I abandoned the diary habit?

Of my remaining years in Washington, till my departure early in 1966, only a few of my notes remain and these have mostly to do with the disastrous Vietnam War which was so soon to darken the Washington scene, to twist and distort political—and sometimes personal—relationships. As anyone who has lived through the last world war knows, a nation at war requires total support from its friends, not qualified approval, still less wise advice from the sidelines. Our Canadian support for the Americans over Vietnam was more explicit than we always recall in retrospect, but it did not meet the demand. As Ambassador in Washington I found myself once again representing a Canadian government that had not come up to American expectations. There was not the acrimony which had marked the Diefenbaker-Kennedy exchanges; the mood now in the White House and the State Department was one of disappointment, a "more in sorrow than in anger" mood, though the anger was to come later. My own official record of this period is embalmed in the archives of the Department of External Affairs. What follows is no comprehensive account of relations between Canada and the United States on the Vietnam War or on any other of the many subjects of negotiation between the two countries during that time. It was compiled from notes taken at the time.

Lyndon Baines Johnson in his solemn hour lumbers to the podium to face his fellow Americans. The portentous utterances are lowered slowly into the waiting world. An

impressively firm yet benevolent statesman enunciates the
purposes and aspirations of the nation. The undertaker's
tailoring encases a hulking, powerful body, something formidable by nature but dressed up and sleeked down. The
President is not to be mocked. His displacement—as they say
of ocean liners—is very great. He is a man of Faith, a man of
ideals and of sagacity, and above all a man of power. No
greater power has been in history than in this incarnation. He
is our nuclear shield, leader of the West, dispenser of aid,
sender of satellites, spender of billions, arbiter of differences,
hurler of thunderbolts. The President of the United States of
America! Foreign ministers and potentates gather at his gates.
"How did you get on with the President?" That is the
question, and woe betide the one who fails to pass the test. If
the Jovian countenance fell into sullen furrows, then no more
loans—no more arms. The chill spreads rapidly through the
furthest confines of the administration. Lips tighten all down
the line to the humblest desk officer in the State Department.
What it is to be in the Presidential Doghouse! I have been
there once or twice—or my country has. They are still civil in
the government offices—civil and chilly—but give them a
drink or two after dinner and it all comes out with rough
frankness. Your government has erred and strayed from the
way and the sheep-dogs are at your heels barking you back
into line. Disagreeable it is at times—even offensive. Your
Prime Minister may be harshly censured, but a word of
criticism of the President of the United States of America and
the heavens would fall with a weight appalling to contemplate.

Even when the sun of favour is shining, there are outer
limits for a foreigner to exchanges of thought with the
Washington higher management. For one thing, the President never listens—or at any rate never listens to foreigners.
He talks them down inexhaustibly. The phrase "consultations with allies" is apt to mean, in United States terms,

briefing allies, lecturing allies, sometimes pressuring allies or sounding out allies to see if they are sound. The idea of learning anything from allies seems strange to official Washington thinking. The word comes from Washington and is home-made.

When LBJ first came to power—in those few months when he counted none but well-wishers in Washington—that good friend of Canada, Scotty Reston expounded to me the pleasing notion that, as the new President was inexperienced in international affairs and as Mike Pearson was an international figure, there could be a fruitful and friendly working relationship between them. The President would turn to Mike for advice as a neighbour, one he could trust in a homely dialogue across the fence. It did not work out like that—perhaps it could never have been expected to do so. When Mike Pearson came on his first official visit to Washington there was little stirring of interest in the White House. The President had much to occupy him; the visit seemed treated as of marginal importance. The Prime Minister's opening speech under the portico of the White House consisted largely in a heartfelt tribute to J. F. Kennedy—natural, inevitable so soon after the assassination, but not particularly heartwarming to the President. The President responded by a reference to our "undefended border". At dinner at the Canadian Embassy the President seemed bored. The Canadian government's gift of an RCMP English-type saddle brought a mumble that it "had no pommel". One saw it relegated to the White House attic. Yet the Prime Minister was not easily discouraged. He was determined to break through the ice and melt it with his charm and humour. He succeeded—or appeared to succeed. Before the visit to Washington was over he had had a long, private talk with the President which put the two of them on a footing of frankness. The President was genial and gossipy.

There followed an invitation to the Pearsons to go to the

presidential ranch for the weekend. What effect—if any—this further intimacy had on the President is unknown. The ranch life seemed to the Pearsons a sort of burlesque circus. The hookers of bourbon at all hours, the helicoptering to visit neighbours, the incessant telephoning, the showing off, the incoherence and inconsequence of the arrangements—all disconcerted Mike. What disconcerted him even more was the impossibility of having any continuous discussion with the President, any exploration of political questions. The President was free with some fairly scabrous gossip about his fellow Senators. He would unexpectedly throw across to the Prime Minister a secret telegram or report which he was reading—thus making a demonstration of the easy, trustful way he felt about him, but there was none of that exchange of views on international or bilateral matters which had characterized the Prime Minister's meeting with Kennedy at Hyannisport in 1963.

All the same, the visit had been a success in political and personal terms. LBJ appeared to take to Mike and that, in terms of Canada–United States relations, was much gained. Every time the President saw me at an official reception he would send the warmest greetings to the Prime Minister, whom he described to me on one occasion as the head of government he "felt closest to".

Then came the thunderclap. The Prime Minister's speech at Temple University in Philadelphia on April 2, 1965, advocating a pause in the bombing in Vietnam—and the President's reaction to it—are part of political history, and this is not an historical record. The President's reception of the speech was sulphurous, and the relationship between the two men never fully recovered. No doubt LBJ believed that an attempt had been made by one he thought to be a friend "to dictate United States policy in his own backyard". When the Prime Minister arrived in Philadelphia he found a telegram from the President inviting him to lunch at Camp

David. The telegram had been dispatched before the President had read the text of the speech. I accompanied the Prime Minister to Camp David—an occasion unfortunately unforgettable. Presidential aides Mac Bundy and Jack Valenti met us at the little airfield—no President. They were like schoolboys escorting the victim to the headmaster's study for a sharp wigging or possibly "six of the best". With strange innocence the Prime Minister and I were not fully prepared for what was to come. We anticipated that the speech would not be popular. Indeed, the Prime Minister's expressed reason for not consulting the President in advance of making it had been that LBJ might put pressure on him to excise the reference to a pause in the bombing.

Camp David could be a cozy mountain retreat—with a large, rough stone fireplace and the kind of pictures that go with it—but it was not cozy that day. LBJ received us with a civility that only gradually began to seem a trifle cool. I noticed with mild surprise that, contrary to his custom, he drank only one Bloody Mary before lunch. I made so bold as to have two. At luncheon the general conversation was made impossible because the President talked almost continuously on the table telephone. Part of the time he was receiving reports on bombing operations in Vietnam, at other times he seemed to be tidying up any telephone calls remaining at the bottom of his list—some fairly trivial ones that could have waited. Mike was left to make conversation with Lady Bird, Mac Bundy, and myself. He talked of the day's flight over the battlefield of Gettysburg, of his long interest in the battle and in the civil war in general. Lady Bird was receptive—he made a joke and she distinctly smiled. Mac and I at intervals made a remark.

Lunch was over and there had been no mention of the speech. Over coffee the Prime Minister took the leap. "What," he inquired, "did you think of my speech?" The President paused before replying. It was the pause when darkest clouds lower, pregnant with the coming storm. "Awful," he said, and taking Mike by the arm, he led him onto the terrace.

What followed I witnessed mainly in pantomime, although from time to time the President's voice reached us in expletive adjuration. He strode the terrace, he sawed the air with his arms, with upraised fist he drove home the verbal hammer blows. He talked and talked—phrases reached Mac and me as we stood fascinated, watching from the dining room which gave onto the terrace through the open French windows—expostulating, upbraiding, reasoning, persuading. From time to time Mike attempted a sentence—only to have it swept away on the tide. Finally Mac suggested that he and I should take a walk through the wooded hills and leave our two masters together.

Our conversation was a reproduction in minor key of what we had just been witnessing. Mac, with the gentleness of a deft surgeon, went for the crucial spots. Perhaps, he suggested, he had not got his message across to me in our last conversation when he had reminded me of the undesirability of public prodding of the President. (I had in fact conveyed this message to Ottawa.) Why had the Prime Minister chosen the United States as the place for such a speech? Why had there been no prior consultation with the President? Did I realize that the Prime Minister's plea for a pause in the bombing coming at this time might inhibit the very aim he had in mind? The tone was friendly but the scalpel was sharp. I countered by saying that the substance of the speech was a Canadian policy statement and in our view a wise one. The Prime Minister was speaking as a Nobel Prize lecturer at an academic occasion; he must deal with issues affecting the peace of the world. The thought of interfering in United States policy was far from his mind. Finally, losing patience with unanswerable questions about the choice of place and occasion, I added that I could assure him that the United

States would never have a better or more understanding friend than the present Prime Minister.

By this time we had wound our way back again to the house. In the dining room we found Jack Valenti. The three of us looked out again at the terrace—the two figures were still there and the drama seemed to be approaching a climax of physical violence. Mike, only half seated, half leaning on the terrace balustrade, was now completely silent. The President strode up to him and seized him by the lapel of his coat, at the same time raising his other arm to the heavens.* I looked at Mac in consternation, but he was smiling. "It will be all right now," he said, "once the President has got *it* off his chest." Shortly thereafter LBJ and the Prime Minister re-entered the house and we took our departure. The President this time accompanied the Prime Minister to the airport and parted with him with geniality.

That night when I got back to Washington I rang up the Prime Minister, who had returned to Ottawa. I was emotional. I said to him that I had never been prouder of him than now. Indeed, he was both right and courageous in what he said, and the President would have done well to listen.

Some weeks later I was lunching with the indomitable Dean Acheson, who attacked Mike and referred critically to his speech. Once again I explained the background and defended the substance. "Oh," said Dean, "you will see that bouncy man come back here and do it again."

The next year when the Prime Minister received the Atlantic Pioneer Award of Federal Union Incorporated at Springfield, Illinois, he made a speech dealing with issues involving the relationship between the United States and its NATO allies. The speech was thought in Washington to

---

*It has been stated that the President grabbed the Prime Minister by the back of the shirt collar and held him off the ground. I saw nothing of the kind and do not believe that this ever happened. It would indeed have been an intolerable insult.

imply some measure of criticism of U.S. attitudes. Again rumbles reached us from the White House. Ambassador-at-Large Averell Harriman was sent to Ottawa to seek clarification. At the White House, Walt Rostow, who had succeeded Bundy, spoke of the Prime Minister's "egregious" speech and of the President's displeasure and "Why," he asked, "did he come into the President's own backyard to make such a speech?"

I heard myself replying much as I had to Mac Bundy on the earlier occasion a year before. But I thought I might guess the answer. Perhaps the Prime Minister had neither forgiven nor forgotten his encounter with the President on the terrace at Camp David. As Dean Acheson remarked, he was "a bouncy man" and he had bounced right back.

London

1967-1971

When in 1966 I left Washington it was to go as Canadian Ambassador and Permanent Representative to the North Atlantic Council in Paris. It seemed that this would be an appropriate and enjoyable assignment. I had had a long experience in matters affecting NATO, dating back to the early days of the Alliance. I had been a student in Paris, and later served in our Embassy there, and I looked forward to returning to a city I loved. As it turned out, I was not a very effective member of the Council and could not recapture the Paris of my younger days. I saw it as a beautiful and historic city that had, in some mysterious way, "come unstuck" in my imagination, an old love revisited when we had little left to say to each other.

In my working life, I succeeded an old friend, George Ignatieff, who had brought enthusiasm and energy to the task. I had neither. Perhaps the strenuous years at the United Nations and in Washington had temporarily drained them out of me. Also, I found the North Atlantic Council itself a curiously unsatisfactory body, despite the able men who composed it. The work itself, covering as it does all aspects of the Alliance, could not fail to be interesting and important, but one had a sense of remoteness from the real centres of power in the NATO capitals where the decisions were reached. A complicating factor for a Canadian Representative was the policy which our government had adopted in relation to France. De Gaulle had pulled the French military forces out of NATO while France still, of course, remained a member of the Alliance. The French action was resented by other NATO governments. The Canadian government, however, partly for understandable domestic reasons, was anxious that the links with France should be maintained and that the French should be made to feel that while we regretted their decision, nothing should be done to widen the breach between France and her NATO allies. This attitude was not popular with the other members of the Council, who tended to see it as a form of appeasement which the French had done nothing to merit. I do not think that the French government much appreciated our efforts. Indeed, Hervé Alphand, then at the head of the Quai d'Orsay (and an old acquaintance of mine from the days when we had both served in Washington), seemed to regard our efforts to placate General de Gaulle with a certain amount of cynical amusement.

Meanwhile, the decision to move the Council from Paris to Brussels had been taken. The Canadian government and its Representative were not favourable to the change— the government on grounds of policy, its Representative on grounds of preference. Although Paris might no longer cast the same spell of illusion, it was still highly agreeable. We had a charming flat, a genius cook, interesting colleagues, and varied friends. The ministerial sessions of the Council gave one an opportunity to see the Foreign Ministers of NATO in action; the discussions in the Council touched on issues affecting the political balance of the Western world and of East-West relations. My daily walks in the Bois de Boulogne were a pleasure. But I had my eye on London. The tenure of Lionel Chevrier as High Commissioner was nearing its close. There was a possibility of a political appointment; on the other hand, a professional diplomat might be chosen. In the event, when Mike Pearson appointed me I felt it to be a recognition that the hand I had played in Washington had not, after all, been so badly played. More than that, I felt it a gesture of friendship from one who was reticent in expressing friendship. I was grateful not only for the appointment but for the friendship.

I had very much wanted the London posting. Who would not? It is, to use a detestable adjective, a "prestigious" appointment. The attractions are obvious: to reside in London in a fine house, to be given the entry to varied English social and political worlds. I had reason to be delighted with my good fortune. It was to be my last post before retirement and I looked forward to it in a spirit best expressed by my friend Douglas LePan, who wrote, in congratulation, that my motto should be that of the Renaissance Pope—"God has given us the Papacy, now let us enjoy it."

London meant something more for me than my official position. As a child in Nova Scotia it was the London of Dickens which merged with my mother's stories of her own London experiences to create in my imagination a multitudinous city, the only scene for the full spectacle of life. When I was a schoolboy in England, London was the promised land at the end of term, the cornucopia of theatres and treats. When I was an undergraduate at Oxford, London meant the Big World where one's friends sank or swam when thrust out into the business of earning a living. Later still, I myself was to be one of these, a fledgling journalist on the *Evening Standard*, living in a bed-sitting room above a grocer's shop in the Earls Court Road. London had by then become a work place, seen without illusion, as familiar as an old shoe. Coming back to it in war was a different matter. Under the bombs, one had a fellow feeling for every passerby in the streets. War and shared danger gave birth to a sense of community which peace had never achieved. We pitied those who were not with us in London in those days.

So, with memories tugging at my elbow, here I was back once again; back, but with a difference. Before I had, as a Canadian, slipped in and out of the interstices of English life. Recognized in no social category, I had the freedom of the city; I was familiar without belonging, an insider-outsider. Now I came as the official representative of Canada, tagged and classified, also handsomely housed. The residence of the Canadian High Commissioner—12 Upper Brook Street—was originally a typical upper-class town house. It had been bombed out during the war and was largely reconstructed. The result was satisfactory, but somehow lacked conviction, like a woman with a face-lift.

There was ample space for entertainment; the rooms were shapely and spacious. The long drawing-room had originally been decorated in glowing colours with rich fabrics imported from Paris. Later the Anglo-Saxon taste of some of the incumbents had been unable to stomach these splendours and had opted for middle-brow beige and genteel lime green in curtains and coverings. The pictures were a mixed bag—Canadian artists rubbing shoulders, not always happily, with their English neighbours, a Group of Seven iceberg staring blankly at a Mortlake tapestry of cupids disporting themselves in a pillared pleasance.

It required five servants to run the house. Of these, the butler was paid by the government, the cook and the maids out of my allowances. As to the fare provided there, the food—as always, under my wife's direction—was excellent. An inspired cook herself, she knew the difference. The wines were passable. The dinner table accommodated thirty, the drawing rooms comfortably up to three hundred. The chauffeur, John Rowan, and his wife and son had an agreeable apartment in the basement. John was, and is, a remarkable man. He accommodated himself with tact, while preserving his own complete independence, to a succession of High Commissioners, each one very different from his predecessor. The official car was the largest, most indecently ostentatious vehicle to be seen in London. (It has since been sold to an undertaking firm and must add class to any funeral, rivalling the hearse in length and gloomy grandeur.)

My office in Canada House was on a scale to match the car. It had been the dining room of the old Union Club from whom the Canadian government had originally purchased the building. I knew the room well from the years when Vincent Massey had been High Commissioner and I, as his private secretary, inhabited the adjacent cubbyhole. How often had I trod the acres of carpet that separated the entrance from the outsize desk behind which the small figure of the High Commissioner was seated. How often had I stood looking over his shoulder while he peered dubiously at the drafts of speeches I had written for him. It was under the great chandelier that hung from the middle of the ceiling that he had stood when, in 1939, he had announced to the staff Canada's declaration of war. Vincent Massey had been a distinguished representative of Canada. He was a well-known and respected figure in political, social, and artistic circles in London. He had dignity without pomposity, intelligence and charm. Here I now was in his place; it remained to be seen what I could make of it.

The times had changed, and so had the relationship between Britain and Canada. In the days of Vincent Massey the Canadian government, under the leadership of Mackenzie King, was obsessed by the suspicion that Whitehall was plotting designs against our nationhood and trying to draw us back into the imperial framework. Our attitude, however, was ambiguous, as Mackenzie King himself demonstrated when he chose as the title for his own book on Canada's war effort, *Canada at Britain's Side*.

Now, in 1967, the ambiguity had been resolved, but what had taken its place? We no longer harboured fears of British dominance. We had finally emerged from the motherhood of the British Empire, only to struggle for breath in the brotherly embrace of Uncle Sam. There were still enduring ties, rooted in history and common institutions, which gave Britain a special place in the affection of Canadians—at any rate of Anglo-Canadians. We were allies in NATO, fellow members of the Commonwealth, owing allegiance to the same Queen. There was extensive trade between us; there were innumerable special links between groups—professional, business, and cultural. Every spring, London was inundated by our fellow countrymen. They came for the historic sights, for the theatre, for the charms of London and the English countryside, sometimes to visit scenes where they had served in the war or for reunions with friends and relatives. The affection for England was there, but British influence was gone. No future Prime Minister was ever likely to call his book *Canada at Britain's Side*. We and the British were excellent friends who had known each other for a long time, but we were no longer members of the same family. If our attitudes had changed, so had those of the British. With their loss of influence had come some loss of interest. Canadians were well liked in England, Canada was esteemed. There remained the bonds of the past, but our future was no longer any concern of theirs. If our preoccupations were with the United States, theirs were increasingly with Europe.

The relations between the Canadian and the British governments in the years when I was in London were, for the most part, untroubled, or, as they say in official communiqués, "cordial and friendly". They offered no challenges or ordeals to a Canadian High Commissioner. After Washington, this was a rest cure. The drama was not in London, it was in Paris. It was French policy, with its impact on the future of Quebec, that was of absorbing interest to the Canadian government.

The advent of Pierre Trudeau as Prime Minister in April 1968 did not affect our relationship with the United Kingdom. There was a very different style and a shift of emphasis, not of policy. Mike Pearson was well known and liked in London. He was also a strong supporter of the Commonwealth and of NATO. Trudeau at first showed no great enthusiasm for either. While his somewhat flamboyant behaviour on his first visit to England in January 1969 got plenty of press notice, his official contacts with the United

Kingdom government went smoothly and satisfactorily. He and the Prime Minister, Harold Wilson, got on well together. It gradually became apparent that, despite the talk then prevalent in government circles in Ottawa of our military withdrawal from NATO, nothing of the sort was seriously contemplated; also, the Canadian government would continue to play a positive role in Commonwealth affairs. Nor did the coming to power of the Conservative government in Britain in 1971 make any real difference to Canadian–United Kingdom affairs. The new Conservative Foreign Secretary was Alec Home. I had never experienced anything but friendliness from George Brown when he held that office in the Labour government, but Alec Home was quite exceptional in his wisdom, tolerance, and charm. Our day-to-day relations with the Foreign and Commonwealth Office were conducted with Dennis Greenhill, an effective and sensible realist. At Buckingham Palace the Queen's secretary, Michael Adeane, I had known since Ottawa days when he had been an A.D.C. at Government House. One of the most astute of men, he is also the best of friends.

In Marlborough House, the seat of the Commonwealth Secretariat, the Canadian Secretary-General, Arnold Smith, a former colleague in the Department of External Affairs, deployed his enthusiasm, skill, and patience in dealing with problems more difficult and demanding than those which faced the High Commissioner.

There was a large and competent staff at Canada House, among whom I counted some very good friends. It often occurred to me that the place could function quite satisfactorily without any High Commissioner at all. The atmosphere of the office was congenial. I had with me, in Geoff Murray, Jerry Hardy, and Louis Rogers, very able Deputy High Commissioners. We had entered a new age of administration. The monstrous growth of regulations, the avalanche of forms and bureaucratic paraphernalia, created a jungle in which I was lost. I had been trained in a simpler era when External Affairs was smaller. The change was inevitable, but I could not get away from the conviction that self-regulating bureaucracy took up too much time which should have been devoted to the formulation and execution of policy. There was too much harness and no bloody horse! Louis Rogers, who had come to Canada House after being our Ambassador to Israel, understood both policy and administration. He controlled his impatience with my administrative ineptitude and enlivened the working hours by his sardonic wit. His wife June was stimulating in talk, lovely to look at, the daughter of my old chief, Hume Wrong. I had known her since she was a child.

As there were few policy questions at issue between our two governments, the functions of the High Commissioner were largely those of a representative and a reporter. There were speeches to be made and ceremonial occasions to attend. There was also the multifarious daily business involved in our close trade, cultural, immigration, and tourist relations with the United Kingdom. There were frequent—all too frequent—visits of Canadian Cabinet Ministers and delegations of officials; there were press conferences and briefings. There were close contacts to be maintained with the Agents General of the provinces in London, and with the Canadian colony there.

There was reporting on the British political and economic situation for the inattentive ears of Ottawa. There are few echoes of these reports in the London diaries, which reflect a varied and lively social life and scarcely dwell at all on the public events which formed the substance of dispatches to Ottawa now lying dormant in the files of the Department of External Affairs.

The years I spent as High Commissioner in London, although enjoyable personally, were not an inspiriting period in British history. The country was wracked by strikes and industrial disputes. Under uninspired political leadership the nation seemed increasingly fragmented, with every group pursuing its own particular interests. Yet the notion that England was a "sick society" was a superficial judgement. The country was indeed suffering from social and economic ailments which took forms peculiar to England. But the disease was to spread to other industrialized nations, including our own. Throughout the stresses and strains of these years the underlying strength of British character and British institutions remained intact. The English themselves were—as they had always been—kindly, ironic, and stoical. Britain remained one of the most civilized countries in the world, if civilization is to be judged by standards of tolerance and humanity.

October 2, 1967
London is a fever of hope deferred. Some day (?) I shall get on top of this job, lead my own life, make my mark. What mark? A first-class reporter who knows all and everyone; a counsellor whose counsel is sought; host at a present-day Holland House; loved but not inconveniently, sought after but not pressed, liked and respected by my own government but at a distance; no more ministerial visits; good cook, interesting books, no chocolate-covered chairs in the "guest suite"; reputation of a brilliant speaker but never having to justify it by making any more speeches; taken as natural by the young.

October 6, 1967
Yesterday was quite different. I walked in Hyde Park under a cloudy sky. Damp oozed from the grass beneath my feet. I carried an old borrowed umbrella, tied together with a rubber band. I had just been reading Virginia Woolf's *Mrs. Dalloway*. It had reopened a way of feeling and seeing that belonged to its time—an anarchic mixture of exhilaration and sadness. As the seagulls scattered and swooped over the park expanses, restlessness and dead wishes stirred. I thought, too,

of Life (and we know how Virginia Woolf loved talking of Life).

I went into the Griffin in Villiers Street, near Charing Cross Station, to meet Elizabeth [Bowen]. It is perhaps to become our London equivalent of the Plaza Bar in New York. We sat drinking, talking, and eating cold beef sandwiches. She looked—and was—extraordinarily young (there must have been some quality in the day that made it a pocket in time, a day out of the steady progression). She began to talk about the figures of Bloomsbury she had known in her youth—Virginia Woolf, the Stracheys. It was a sudden outbreak of her old brilliant, individual, visual talk, which has been muted lately. She made me see the ingrowingness of that little Bloomsbury world, their habit of writing endless letters to each other, of analysing, betraying, mocking, envying each other. She spoke of the kind of pains of jealousy and treachery which they inflicted on each other. She thinks that that kind of intellectual, professional, upper middle-class, like the Stracheys, tends more to corruption than any other class and that, in that sense, they are "clogs to clogs". Elizabeth is approaching the last chapter of *Eva Trout*. God knows how it will be received. Her delight in it is catching. The people she can't now bear are those who say nostalgically to her, "I did so love *The Death of the Heart*."*

In the afternoon a Brigadier and his wife came for drinks, she a tiresome woman with that air of tucking away what you say to her with disapproval, as if she would take it out of her bag when she got home and, if necessary, report it to the Proper Authorities.

October 27, 1967
Went to Colchester for the Colchester oyster feast. Rather fun, these little excursions and getting glimpses of the endless

*First published in 1938.

groupings of English life. This week the Distillers in the city, and the Warrant Holders' Banquet, and now this little world of Colchester. All the local worthies and bigwigs—Ted Heath,* who made a speech and spoke of the typically Essex faces in the audience. I looked down from the high table at the long, pale faces with very pale blue eyes and colourless hair and total lack of expression—Essex types? It rained. I don't care for Colchester oysters and I noticed that neither the Mayor nor the Aldermen touched them. I sat next Lady Allport, wife of the man who heads the Mission to Rhodesia, and did not charm her, which was a pity as she did rather charm me. Next to her, on her other side, was the head of the Boilermakers' Union, whom she described as a "very cozy character".

November 1, 1967
Popski's attitude towards us has changed since his long incarceration in kennels during the quarantine period on his arrival in England. I think we made a mistake in visiting him when he was caged up in the kennels. He greeted us with frantic excitement, but when we walked away from him he was in despair. I believe that he came to think that we had deserted him and never forgave us.

Since he has been released and come to this house, he lives by preference most of the time in the kitchen. When we call him he comes, allows himself to be patted for a moment, is perfectly polite to us as though we were distant acquaintances. I am sure he bears us a deep grudge for—as he thinks—abandoning him in prison.

November 5, 1967
It is at this precise time—11 a.m.—that Sylvia is going into the operating room. She fell day before yesterday and broke

*Edward Heath—then Leader of the Opposition, subsequently Conservative Prime Minister.

her hip. The doctors said that she could either remain in bed for six weeks without moving, so that the bones might heal naturally, or have a pin put in to hold them together. She chose the latter, as she couldn't bear the prospect of the total inaction. I am unreasonably nervous and depressed about this operation, which I am told is quite a routine one. How much she means to me, and how lonely I should be without her, how much married I have become. The thought of the actual operation sickens me. The weather is depressingly black, the house deadly silent (this house, like the house where Lytton Strachey spent his youth, has developed elephantiasis, disproportionate swollen growth).

November 6, 1967

I went to the banquet in the Guildhall given for the President of Turkey and sat next Mrs. Mulley, who is the wife of the Minister of State at the Foreign Office. Her husband was a Cambridge don, but it bored him, so now he is a politician. How does one make that transition? Politicians always seem to me a race apart, like actors, and I am surprised to find that they nearly all once plied ordinary trades. The laundry had sent someone else's shirt back and I wore a collar sizes too big for me, but no one knew or cared.

Sylvia has come out of the operation. It has gone very well. She was already sitting up a few hours after regaining consciousness and asking for *newspapers*.

November 21, 1967

Mike Pearson has arrived, and Maryon. I felt such affection, attraction, for them when I saw them arriving at the airport. He seems happy at being here, and young—much younger than I am. Lunch with Blair Fraser* at the Travellers. This was my day for liking people, although I have always liked

*Canadian journalist.

him and find him admirable. With us elderlies much depends on the day, state of fatigue, health, etc. We have our recoveries, and can be almost human.

Mike's press conference very dreary; it dragged and he knew it. The British press uninterested—no angle for them.

January 3, 1968—Doodles to replace a diary
I can pray for myself but it seems a presumption to pray for others.

" 'Damn' braces, 'bless' relaxes"—Blake.

I cling to rationalization like a man hanging on to his pants to prevent them falling down.

The burrows of the nightmare, the stuff that dreams are made of; endless riches piled in those caves of sleep, mixed with rubbish and wildly comical juxtapositions. This is what Bunuel is after in his films, and catches, and the lewd delights!

The Turner Venetian scene over the fireplace "floods the room with colour"—and it does.

Wheeler-Bennett would be the best to do Vincent Massey's biography, but he cries out for Proust, a Canadian Proust.

Is there any point in balancing one's prejudices with "fair-mindedness"? Why not turn purple with prejudice and passion, make no allowance? Why not give way to envy, and to blind loyalty too? Come on, join the human race.

January 20, 1968
Garwood, the butler, has his endearing side, also an infuriating side. Last evening I said to him, "General Anderson would like a dry martini *on the rocks.*" He made a martini with ice *in the shaker* and poured it. I said, "That is not a martini on the rocks." He said, "Yes, sir, it's just the same, *not to worry*. I have a reputation for my martinis." "I was

restrained from pursuing the argument by the presence of a guest" (as Mr. Pooter* would have said), but the guest, Bill Anderson, said when Garwood had left the room, "He certainly won the battle of the rocks." I laughed, pretty grudgingly. As a General, Bill has a sharp eye for victories and defeats.

Garwood and Popski make a pair. I don't know how two such egotists get on together. Garwood recognizes Popski's tactical skills, sometimes calling him "the General" or "Your Royal Highness", at others addressing him good-humouredly as "you silly old fool". Popski has been given the stone out of an avocado pear and will not let anyone go near him in case they try to take it away from him. He bangs it on the parquet floor, making a considerable racket for a small dog with a small object.

January 21, 1968
Beryl Saul and her two sons are staying here. Her husband, Bill, who was my Military Adviser in Paris and of whom I was fond, died suddenly two weeks ago at forty-eight years old of a cerebral haemorrhage. She is in a state of shock. Her eldest son is a parachutist in the British Army, just back from Aden. His batman was shot in the back by an Arab terrorist. "He was the most innocent boy I ever saw, wouldn't have hurt a fly. What were we fighting for in Aden anyway? Was it worth his life?" The second Saul boy wants to join the Department of External Affairs. Both had been brought up in the Canadian military tradition, as of course was Bill Anderson, who dined with us last night. So we have been seeing quite a lot of the Canadian military. They are the descendants of the old Canadian Permanent Force, the class and kind of people I was accustomed to in Halifax in my youth—Canadians modelled on a British tradition.

*Mr. Pooter is a character in *Diary of a Nobody*, by George Grossmith.

January 22, 1968
Called on Polish Ambassador in the morning. He is pessimistic about British recovery. He says that the United Kingdom has for years had the lowest rate of investment in Europe, so there is no base for a recovery founded on the export drive. England, he says, is hampered by her class system and is not drawing upon all the human material available in the country. I questioned this latter bit but I don't know if I am right. This seems to me a democratic society, but what does one mean by that? British society seems pulverized, its different segments living unto themselves, innumerable private pockets and groups and individual interests. The only solidarity seems to be that of the young against the old, and vice versa.

I got Hardy* to qualify the gloom of his telegram about Wilson's future as Prime Minister. It is too easy to be carried away by these gusts of opinion. Wilson is not through yet, though many I meet wish he were.

Lunched alone on sausages and mash at the Griffin—"There is a table free, love, in the corner."

Went to the National Gallery and saw a celestially blue Bellini Madonna, "such a forgiving blue" as Stephen Tennant would have said. John Maher says the National Gallery is too near to go to and I am going to prove the opposite.

March 10, 1968
Reflections on a spring Sunday afternoon . . . The picture of the world from the TV and the Sunday papers is an apocalyptic one—race war, war between the generations, collapse of the financial system, Vietnam, collapse of moral values, erosion of parliamentary government, etc., etc. America in trauma, England full of self-disgust, and everywhere swarms of protesting students—in Warsaw, Cambridge, Tokyo, Rome, in America, Canada, in China, in Europe—hordes of

*J. E. G. Hardy—Deputy High Commissioner.

angry milling masses of placard-bearing youth. Student riots—a preliminary to revolution? What kind of revolution? Against what, and for what? The casualties or near-casualties of this day in time include internationalism (the decline of the United Nations and the Commonwealth), the multiracial society (racial struggle in America, in England, and now in Kenya), the concept of "one world" (nationalism is everywhere rampant). Is some vast shudder going through the frame of man-made society or is it all inflated and inflamed by the news media?

Today Sylvia and I went in this mild grey weather for a mild and happy little expedition to Richmond. We walked along the tow-path, past dilapidated hotels, to the Star and Garter, where we had lunch for only £1.10 and looked out on the famous view of the bend of the river. Then we took a mini-taxi to Ham House.* How strange it is, unlike any other house in the world. To think of that coarse, sinister, scheming couple—the Lauderdales—plotting in these little over-decorated rooms among the japanned cabinets in the baroque décor under the floridly painted ceilings. Ghosts that Horace Walpole said, when he visited the house in 1770, he would not give sixpence to see. One would give more than sixpence *not* to see them.

March 11, 1968

I wonder, sometimes, about my various predecessors in this house. I suppose they had the same marital conversations about servants and allowances, plus talk, in their case, of their children, and they made love in the same bed and looked out at the same chimney-pots and ended by "loving London".

I was so touched and pleased that Peter† came with a present of six pairs of silk stockings for Sylvia. I recognized

*Ham House, Richmond, Surrey—originally the home of Lord Lauderdale, Scottish politician in the reign of Charles II.

†Peter Elliston, an old friend from boyhood in Halifax.

him in this gesture more than anything he has done since I met him again. He told Sylvia that he had come to see me because I sounded so low on the telephone.

March 12, 1968
Frederic Hudd* died last night. At the end, he said that he wished he had married, and that he had had a lonely life. General and Mme Ailleret were killed in a plane accident yesterday. Two ways of dying—a stroke following old age and years of senility, or a plane crash. Which would you choose?

Garwood, the butler, is back, "on the wheel" as he puts it. He looks years younger for his illness.

For some reason, when I woke up this morning I was thinking about butlers. I could write a book about "Butlers I Have Known". In their lofty idea of their own position and their devotion to protocol, in the gravity of their public façade, they much resemble certain ambassadors. Indeed, they often look like them physically. On one unlucky occasion at a cocktail party, I called out, rather impatiently, to the passing servitor, "Bring me another whisky, please," only to realize a moment later that he was a newly arrived Ambassador of notorious prickliness and self-importance. However, butlers can get their own back as effectively as diplomats. Once, at a reception in Ottawa, I encountered an ex-butler from one of our embassies, now—with his wife—catering for parties there. An old Cockney he was. He greeted me with the remark, "I just said to my wife when I saw you: 'My God, how Mr. Ritchie's aged; *my God*, how he has aged!' " I tried to indicate my lack of interest in this train of thought, but he went on repeating it with intense conviction.

April 12, 1968—Weston Hall
Staying with Sachie and Georgia Sitwell for Easter. We had a

*Former Deputy High Commissioner, Canada House.

day at the races with Kisty Hesketh* and her party from Easton Neston. High spirits in a cutting wind at the races. Lunch in a drafty tent—shivered with cold and thoroughly enjoyed myself. Back to Weston for tea (cinnamon toast and chocolate cake).

Now I sit writing in this little bedroom overlooking the garden where first I came twenty-eight years ago, and I remember the intoxication of the first visit when the name Sitwell was a key to a fabulous landscape with figures. Sachie is now recovering from an operation but refuses to be daunted by illness. They have both been so affectionate and welcoming—I love them.

April 20, 1968

We have a new Prime Minister—Trudeau—and I try, from reading articles about him, from talking to his friends, to penetrate to the man. Nothing so far said or printed reveals him to me, nor did my own meeting with him. I recall something enigmatic about him which struck me even at that time, long before his present celebrity, something inhuman (the word is too strong) beneath the courteous, charming manner; too much all-of-a-piece, perhaps, the cultivated, intelligent cool observer?

April 21, 1968

It is time that Elizabeth returned. What if she never did? Some day she won't.

In St. James's Park, sensually happy in the morning, sensually sad in the evening.

Read Malraux's *Anti-Memoirs*. I started it as a duty and was discouraged and surprised to find how many French words I do not understand. Then I read on and something else irritated me—there was too much talk of Destiny. I

---

*Christian, Lady Hesketh.

began to suspect inflation, and a peculiarly French form of inflation, but I persisted and was rewarded, engaged, swept along by the marvellous rhythms of language and brought up short by the telescoping of thought and image.

April 22, 1968

Just back from a week-end staying with Huntley Sinclair for the Badminton Horse Show. Huntley, an old friend from early Ottawa days, came over here in the RCAF during the war and has stayed on and married a very nice and very wealthy woman. They live in a big house of Cotswold grey stone, with a Lutyens wing and a view of the Stroud valley.

The Queen is staying near by with the Duke and Duchess of Beaufort, and was at the morning service in Badminton church. She had a word with me on the way out of church about Trudeau's succession as Prime Minister. (I had told her some days ago that I felt certain that he would win over his competitors.)

The Queen has treated me with the greatest kindness and informality since I have been here. And she has no more devoted admirer than I. It is not only loyalty to the Throne (and I have always been a royalist) but fascination with the personality of the woman who occupies it.

May 2, 1968

What would we do without Jean Halton? She is the widow of Matthew Halton, the brilliant Canadian journalist, and we are lucky enough to have her as social secretary at Canada House. It's a tricky job, as, in addition to our own official entertaining, she has to cope with the stream of applications by Canadian visitors for invitations to the Royal Garden Parties and the Trooping of the Colour. The applicants do not always realize that these invitations have to be shared out among all members of the Commonwealth. Those who do not get invitations sometimes become disgruntled, and Jean copes with these and all other social problems with her mixture of charm, good humour, and friendly firmness.

May 6, 1968
A blowing day of wide skyscapes. Sylvia wore her purple suit with a new flowered blouse and we walked together in Hyde Park, watched a sailing boat capsize in the Serpentine, and came home to lunch on trout and asparagus.

The new Canadian government is apparently contemplating some measure of military withdrawal from Europe and perhaps from NATO itself and putting increased emphasis on the continental defence of North America. I am planning to write a dispatch on this subject and have been thinking it over. One argument for the change would be that it would make us slightly more independent of the United States' continental defence umbrella. At first sight this argument is not impressive. Our additional contribution to continental defence would be a flea-bite. Then there is the fashionable argument that money saved from NATO should go into aid and peace-keeping. There is disillusionment, too, with the failure of the Atlantic Community idea and our concept of Article 2 of the Treaty. Also there is the influence of de Gaulle and the French military pull-out from NATO. Some may even believe that by retreat from NATO we might improve Canadian-French relations and take the French heat off Quebec. After de Gaulle's behaviour in Canada this would be kissing the boot that kicked us. Such appeasement would not affect de Gaulle but only encourage him.

There is also the widespread feeling (how widespread I doubt) that NATO is becoming regarded in Canada as an "old-fashioned" military alliance. The very word "alliance" savours to such critics of power groupings and does not fit with our image of ourselves as "progressive". The further dangerous implication is that it is dated to believe in the political or military aggressiveness of the U.S.S.R., especially in Europe. How far does Trudeau share these notions?

At any rate it seems to me quite unthinkable that we should contemplate leaving NATO in the foreseeable future. A unilateral precipitate announcement of troop withdrawals would be messy but not quite so bad. It would gravely embarrass our NATO allies. A phased redeployment of Canadian forces after consultation with our allies could be justified in terms of an increase in our North American responsibilities. It would be disintegrating in its effects on the Alliance, perhaps pointless in terms of positive results, but not fatal.

May 8, 1968

Went down on the morning train to Hythe to spend the day with Elizabeth.* I was an hour early at Folkestone, so Elizabeth was not there to meet me. I walked in the sun round some playing fields and tulip beds and had a happy drink alone in a pub where skippers off the Folkestone-Boulogne boats were reminiscing. Then Elizabeth called for me in the car and we lunched in the hot sun at the Hotel White Cliffs, at Dover, where the glass-ended lounge looks across to the esplanade, to the equable blue channel and the boats coming in and out. It has always been warm and sunny when we have gone together to Dover and we are always happy there and always have Dover sole and Pouligny-Montrachet for lunch and walk afterwards under the cliffs which look as though they would topple over the line of late-Georgian houses, in one of which my aunt, Lale Darwall, ended her days. Then we walked out on the long pier and the weather changed to grey and the landscape looked "like a photograph", as Elizabeth put it. She said that she remembered in her youth coming back from adventures in France on such a day, to find, with sinking heart, England looking just like that.

In the afternoon I read Lady Cynthia Asquith's diaries

---

*Elizabeth Bowen had bought a house in Hythe, Kent.

about the brothers and lovers and sweethearts who went out to die in the 1914-18 war, while the house parties and flirtations and gossip went on at home, and Ego and Ivo and Basil were on the casualty lists or reported "missing, presumed dead". The sadness and waste of it all and the triviality of the gossip combined to depress me. We have come such a long way since then that for all their worldliness they seem innocent—and brave.

Coming home I stood in the light rain alone at Sandling Station waiting for the train—a little station, probably shortly to be suppressed.

June 5, 1968

A dark, rainy morning. The Pearsons, who have been staying here, will be off to the airport for Canada in a few minutes. The shooting of Bobby Kennedy, with its play-back to the assassination of JFK, has given a nightmarish flavour to the last twenty-four hours. Mike says that people in Canada will be smug about it and will say "it couldn't happen here". It only accentuates one's feeling that Canada must not, shall not, be absorbed into that runaway American society which is like a giant plane out of control.

A quiet last evening of the Pearsons' visit—Sylvia and Maryon playing Russian bank, Mike and I watching soccer on the TV, a brisk argument on the future of NATO after dinner, Mike saying that we *will* withdraw our forces from Europe, that NATO is an "old-fashioned military alliance", that our future lies more in the North American continental sphere. It's this last bit that I find difficult to absorb.

June 19, 1968

London seasonitis. Morning of breathless exhaustion, like a swimmer weakening a long way from land, land being in this case our holiday at Chester. Deterioration of human relations because of always having to break off conversation just as it might come to a point, in order to rush to change for another party. Undue dependence on alcohol to buoy one up for another encounter, smoking frantically in the car in traffic queues, always twenty minutes late for a luncheon or a dinner party; always a day behind in little thank-you notes for a day-before-yesterday's dinner party, or condolence notes to widows whose mates have finally fallen out of the race due to strokes or heart attacks from just one day or night too much; decline of sexual energy from too much social stress—and all this is self-inflicted (All of Us on All of Us), and still there is the whole of July ahead of us.

June 22, 1968

A muggy, claggy day, a day to sit on a park bench wrapped up in a raincoat like an old tramp, with some crumbs to feed the ducks while waiting for the mild drizzle down to come. But in fact I am away, top-hatted, to the commissioning of a Canadian submarine at Chatham, and to pass in review the crew, and to orate from a dais. And Sylvia, very nervous, is to present the Captain of the submarine with a large crest-engraved silver cigarette box. *There*, that is Commander Swiggum at the door, to A.D.C. us, sitting in the car all the way to Chatham, thus imposing a certain measure of chat. Better have a pee now and not have to arrest our great black hearse at some Esso station on the rain-wet road.

July 8, 1968

Back from Stansted after a most enjoyable week-end with Eric and Mary Bessborough.* Eric says that from his bed he sees nothing but tulips. His bedroom is hung with Dutch paintings of tulips and with beautifully articulated water-colour drawings of tulips; in all the vases are more tulips.

---

*The Earl and Countess of Bessborough. Stansted is their country house in Sussex.

Tulips and macaws—not only paintings of macaws, but real live ones. When not infuriated in a cage, biting the hand that feeds them, they fly free in glorious Technicolor from tree to tree, making a wickedly unfriendly noise, but undeniably ornamental. During lunch on the terrace, as I was putting a piece of pâté to my lips, a macaw swooped down and flew away with it.

Peter Ustinov came for lunch. Is he the clown country gentleman in a nineteenth-century novel? Broad, pale, heavy hands; broad Russian nose; mimicry and wit with the very edge that Russians can find for pretensions and affectations. A lumbering, friendly, comical creature who could change mood with the speed of a bear.

July 27, 1968
In the parks, under the sulky sky and on the used-up grass, the couples lie, length to length. They follow an undeviating protocol in their embraces—kiss, kiss, hug, hug, no copulation; hour after hour they entangle thus without culmination but with convulsive twitching of blue-jeaned buttocks. Dotted about in conveniently sited deck chairs, elderly men watch them, uncross their legs and gaze absently at the clouds above. Children throw balls over the recumbent writhers. Tired ladies in ones, or sometimes twos, close their eyes in unsimulated indifference, and adolescents seated in groups discuss over the recumbent bodies whatever it is that adolescents do discuss.

July 30, 1968
Dinner at The Apéritif with Elizabeth. The bartender remembered me from the days more than twenty years ago when I used to go there and sit on a high bar-stool drinking martinis and waiting for Margot, cursing her for always being three-quarters of an hour late and in an accumulating rage which changed in a jiffy to pleasure and relief when her tall

figure finally came through the door with a rush of modish, Mayfair-ish excuses, interlarded with "darlings". Then there was always the promise of the night ahead—a promise often unfulfilled, and put off with the most blatant lies about her visiting sister-in-law, etc., lies which had to be swallowed because I was only a substitute, a filler-in, a role which, apart from the frustration it sometimes involved, really suited me better than being No. 1, with all its claims.

August 1, 1968
I have been thinking about the forthcoming Commonwealth meeting in London and the role of Canada and of Trudeau in it. He is a new figure whose advent will be greeted by British public opinion and by his Commonwealth peers with curiosity and interest. He may be the star of the Conference; the others are mediocrities. The popular press will be after him, his speeches will get a good play. He is in a position to be heard, if he has anything to say. What is his thinking about the Commonwealth? Is he interested? I doubt it.

Will there be a tendency to expect Canada to take on Britain's role? I don't think so—it's plainly impossible. Arnold Smith, as Secretary-General, will want us to take a more positive part, possibly over Rhodesia. So will Nyerere and Kaunda, who flatter and actually believe in us. All this is very tempting—its multiracial quality is popular in Canada; also it corresponds to a real but not deep-rooted trust in Canada by the Africans. But the terrain is dangerous. Expectations can easily be built up and disillusionment can result. The British might be prepared to push us into a more ambitious role. It will cost us more in aid—perhaps we can afford that? We should, in talking to the Africans, not "hot them up" but try to cool them off. There is realism among them underneath. We should not get mixed up in their politics or in the protection of British interests, which a Commonwealth Peace Force would have meant. We should

stay right away from African freedom fighters. We mustn't
be used by Harold Wilson and must remember the possibility that the Conservatives may be in power in England before
long.

Unless we do propose to be the champions of the
Africans and assume a new Commonwealth leadership there
is nothing much in the way of a role for us. Our posture
should be a sensible middle-of-the-way realism, using the
Commonwealth as an opportunity for numerous bilateral
contacts, showing a general disposition that it should continue and being willing to contribute to this end. The
Commonwealth has links in a world where there are not too
many, and can help in finding compromises provided these
are not so illusory as to rebound against their originators. As
to the Monarchy—in the Commonwealth context—it is a
useful limited device.

August 20, 1968—on holiday in Chester, N.S.
This south shore of Nova Scotia with its mixture of small
fishing villages and sea inlets sparkling in sun and wind,
squat white farmhouses sheltered by trees and set in rough
meadows, has a flavour all its own, never pinned on paper by
painter or writer. And the small towns, some with almost as
many wooden churches as there are wooden houses, look a
standing invitation to peace and suggest the alternative of a
life in which retired hours could pass swaying in a hammock
in the shelter of a verandah. Gulls float and settle, a colony of
them on a hillside; solid big-bellied fishermen rear chunky
big-bellied sons who already as children have the promise of
their fathers' strength.

King Street runs down to the sea, quite a steep hill at
the top which descends gradually at the end. On the right-
hand side of the street stands this small shingle house in
which we four people live—Roley and Bunny and ourselves. I
love the house as if it were my own, especially my bedroom,
which I would change for no other. It is absolutely as plain as

an anchorite's cell, with white painted table and dresser, a chair of unpainted wood, a square mirror hanging on the wall which faintly distorts the features, a hard square bed, and that is all, And I am happier here than anywhere. Outside, the tree-lined street; above, the blue of a sea sky and a glimpse of the blue of the sea itself. Sailing boats in the harbour, and the islands beyond—Quaker, Saddle, and, farther away, Tancook, to which the ferry goes twice a day and once on Sunday. In the gardens of Chester grow nasturtiums, in colours that defy their poor-genteel neighbours, the petunias—colours that pierce the eye and make the heart beat faster—gay, brilliant common nasturtiums in borders and bowls, planted round rocks or even telephone poles. By the roadside and at the foot of meadows near the sea are wild roses, smelling of rose, while the tame ones in gardens are scentless.

August 21, 1968
What a curse is the tiresome gambit of "being offended" which infects some people. At any one time you may rely upon it that someone you know is in a state of "being offended" with someone else. The injured party conveys this state by degrees of coolness, huffiness, and standing on dignity. "Being offended" leads to the second stage—Hurt Feelings. It can be most easily softened by a stroke of misfortune suffered by the offender. In that case, the offended one can, magnanimously, forgive all, but the offender must not hope to escape unscathed if he attempts to continue serenely on his way with a casual apology for the offence.

I should know. I have just "offended" an old acquaintance here. I have also burned the bottom of the electric kettle.

August 22, 1968
Suffering from crisis agitation and the sense of being cut off here. I know that I can contribute nothing, but I feel so

restless that I take no more real pleasure in this holiday. The Czech crisis has been the focus of my restlessness. The thought of those brutes of Russians moving into Prague, stamping out individuals and liberties, reimposing that suffocating regime, makes me almost physically sick. I should think some kind of protest must be registered by the helpless U.N. If we have resolutions about "war-mongering Rhodesia" and don't mention the invasion of Czechoslovakia, except under our breath, the U.N. should shut up shop.

August 23, 1968
The holiday is over. From one day to another Chester has lost its charm for me. I know every board in the board wharf—which is rotting and which is firm; I know every knot-hole in the wood; I know each of the six wild roses in the sloping field. If this euphoric peace, rest, and happiness lasted with me for little more than two weeks, what *will* my retirement be like?

August 27, 1968—Ottawa
Back in Ottawa for three days of consultations. Woke early in my small room at the Château Laurier hotel. How is is that the Department of External Affairs always manage, in the friendliest way, to get the worst accommodation in any hotel or on any airline? But my window, which will not open, looks out on the canal locks and, on the other side of the canal, above the screen of trees, the Gothic towers, conical green copper roofs, and iron fretwork pinnacles of the East Block point upwards to an overcast sky. I took my morning walk round the poop-deck of Parliament Hill overlooking the river and towards Eddy's pulp factory and the Gatineau Hills beyond, the same walk I have paced at intervals for thirty-five years, in every weather and at every turning of my career, in decision and indecision, in panic and exhilaration. Parliament Hill has not changed. The only addition to its popula-

tion of frock-coated Victorian statues is a monstrously comic—or comically monstrous—version of Mackenzie King, sculpted apparently in shit in the style favoured in Communist countries at the height of the Stalin epoch. It could be a work of revenge by an inspired enemy.

August 28, 1968—Ottawa
A brilliant early autumn Canadian day. I bolted in to the French-Canadian Roman Catholic cathedral for a few minutes to seek sustenance, only to find myself involved in a funeral service, and escaped just before the corpse. One day in Ottawa has gone a long way towards destroying the health and spirits built up in three weeks in Nova Scotia, and I have yet to have my interview with the Prime Minister.

In the Ottawa "Establishment" there is uneasiness; they don't quite know what to expect from Trudeau. They feel a distinctly cool breeze blowing. Many of them now realize that they are getting older and suspect that they soon may be considered out of date. They cluck nervously.

August 29, 1968—Ottawa
I saw Trudeau yesterday. I was talking in his outer office to his secretary, a young French Canadian, when, by a change in his expression, I realized that someone had glided silently into the room and was standing behind me. I turned, and it was Trudeau, looking like a modern version of the Scholar Gypsy in sandals and open-necked shirt, as if he had just blown in from Haunts of Coot and Hern. He is physically altogether slighter, lighter, smaller than his photographs suggest. His air of youth—or is it agelessness?—is preternatural in a man of forty-eight. It is really impossible to connect him with the Office of Prime Minister. The manner is unaffected and instantly attractive; the light blue eyes ironical and amused, but they can change expression, and almost colour, to a chillier, cooler tone. What is behind all this? After this talk

with him I am not perceptibly nearer the mind or motive. I rely on others. Some speak of his great intelligence, his power of organizing Cabinet; others speak of his pragmatism; yet others of his Thomist cast of thought. The truth is that all are baffled by an enigma, and so also am I.

August 30, 1968—Ottawa

The Prime Minister began our interview by asking me whether I thought that the Department of External Affairs was really necessary and, if so, why? I said that I viewed the Department as an instrument for the protection and advancement of Canadian interests abroad and not as a seminar to discuss abstract policy considerations. I think that Trudeau has got it into his head that the Department is divorced from the real interests of Canada and is embarking on international projects which have no firm basis in Canadian needs, and that this has been characteristic of the Pearson era.

I find the climate in Ottawa very anti-NATO. There is a great deal of talk of neutrality for Canada based on the Swedish model. Marcel Cadieux* is not in favour of these trends and told our new Minister of External Affairs, Mitchell Sharp, that we had "no expert on neutrality" in the Department. The British connection is far from popular. I am told that a visit by the Prime Minister to the United Kingdom might "cover his Anglo-Saxon flank", as he must do some things which will annoy the British.

September 1, 1968—London

Back in London, in a dazed condition after a sleepless night on the plane. This house has an uninhabited look and one sees how quickly, when we are gone permanently, it will take on the featureless face of an official residence. It's partly the way the servants "place" furniture—always in straight lines—

*Under-Secretary of State for External Affairs.

so that a woman's first gesture on coming home is to give sofa and chairs a pull and a push, to bring them into a nest-like form. But there is no wife here to "build a nest", as Sylvia remains in Canada for a few more days. Also, no flowers in the house. I look at London with indifference, and the blank August residential streets show no response. It is hard to believe that only a month ago the place abounded in friends and acquaintances, the telephone rang incessantly, and every post contained notes and invitations.

September 2, 1968—Hythe

A girl got into the railway carriage where I was seated alone waiting for the train to start from Charing Cross. I knew from the instant that she appeared that she felt herself embarking on an adventure, perhaps going to meet a lover. She was pale, dark eyes enlarged with excitement, anticipation, nervousness. (It turned out in later talk that she was on her way to Deal to stay for the first time with her young man and to meet his family.) She was so charged with feeling that at random she shot some arrows in my direction. I closed my eyes in pretended sleep and opened them to find her dark glance looking directly into mine. Then two women got into the carriage and planted themselves for the remainder of the journey, one with elephantine knees.

Elizabeth was waiting for me at the station exit at Folkestone. I heaved my suitcase, heavy with whisky and shoes, into the back of her car and off we drove to Hythe. I find her subdued in mood and wonder if she is ill, exhausted perhaps by her permanent cough. I seem to do all the talking. Do I ever give her a chance? The weather is sunless and cool, with a wind that bangs all the doors in this house.

September 5, 1968—London

Dined with the Hardys and found myself face to face with their son, a boy of eighteen—me at the age when I wrote my early diaries.* I imagined myself skinned alive by his electric eye. What would he write in *his* diary? Myself—a gabbling, infinitely old parrot, quite outside the range of human sympathies. At the same time, his physical shyness was such that he could not bring himself to draw his chair into the group of the conversation and was no doubt cursing himself for his own gaucherie.

September 6, 1968
People talk of a second childhood, but am I having a second adolescence? Sylvia returns tonight, and a good thing too. This bedroom is beginning to stink of self. Walking round Grosvenor Square the other evening I contemplated, as a task for my retirement, the editing of my own diaries. They seem to me at the moment so trivial as to be completely unpublishable, even if they were not full of indiscreet or unpleasant references to "living persons" which would cause hurt feelings.

September 7, 1968
This morning I have been having an early walk in the park. It is blazingly fine and already hot. A couple of youths waking up in their sleeping bags and putting their heads out of their cocoons. I might like to sleep like that in the park all night, coiled up in a sleeping bag. I read some of Harold Nicolson's diaries. Diaries are unlovable things and in the long run put one off the writer.

My young cousin Mary Carscallen has been staying the night and has just left, bubbling with her adventures on the Continent, where she and her girl friend have been roaming. Another pair of adventurers—this time male—hove in view in the persons of another cousin, young Roger Rowley, and his

*Later published by Macmillan of Canada under the title *An Appetite for Life*.

friend Larry O'Brien. These two sports have shaken the dust of Rockcliffe from their feet and are questing.

I have been looking, for the first time in years, at my old diaries. They summon up for me impressions, memories, colours, rooms, faces, which are not visible on the written page. It is like reading a play which *I* have seen acted with the original cast and others have never seen.

Dinner at the Painted Hall, Greenwich, for Finance Ministers. Reception at the Banquet Hall, Whitehall, for Athlone scholars. Lunch at the Beefsteak.

September 25, 1968
The Burmese Ambassador called and kept on saying, "Difficult world; very, very difficult," and sighing. Burma probably has plenty to sigh about.

Went to Gatwick Airport to meet our Minister of Finance, Benson. Reception for them here in the afternoon. I made a presentation of Canadian books to the University of Birmingham's representatives and had them to tea. Nice librarians—another world, full of intrigue too. Read Powell's *Afternoon Men* and was back in my own twenties. Did Time ever string ahead indefinitely like that—time to be endlessly wasted, time for interminable hesitations and endless conversations?

October 1, 1968—Plymouth
Sylvia and I are here on an official visit to Plymouth. We are staying in this house which used to be Lady Astor's and has been left to Plymouth on condition that nothing in it should be changed. Every snapshot remains in place, and her copies of the works of Mary Baker Eddy, with salient passages underlined in red by her. An old housekeeper, Florrie, who dates from the Astor regime, goes with the house, which is in a terrace facing on Plymouth Hoe and the sea beyond. The house, although not a bit ghostly, gives one a soothing

sensation which could also be stifling—a sensation of silence and immobility. Everything, once and for all, sealed into its place. This seems all the stranger when one looks at the faded photographs of civic occasions which line the walls and in which the figure of Nancy Astor, like an electric marionette, seems always to be springing about in gesticulation or protest. It is odd to think of that disturbance which must perpetually have swept through this house being displaced by this dead calm of ticking clocks and great cow-like objects of mahogany furniture. I find that to leave the house is like pulling oneself with effort out of a quicksand which could engulf one.

Well, we shall be gone in five minutes, and the Plymouth episode over. Mayor and Mayoress, store managers and newspaper editors, the librarian and the city clerk, will all vanish down a hole in my memory and only the feeling of this silent house facing the level grey sea will remain, and a sense of old-fashioned comfort and permanence which could change to one of being walled up, breathless, in the past.

October 16, 1968
St. James's Park on a fine autumn morning. The pelicans flapping their great wings in the sun and yawning at each other (at least it looks like a yawn—it may be part of a courtship ritual for all I know). I have been rereading those diaries written when I was eighteen. They have stripped away layers of accumulated experience and exposed nerves which I thought dead but which are all too much alive. I started reading them with detachment, but I soon wanted to change them, to leave out this or that which just would not fit in with my later edition of my own youth. Then I began to realize that I was not reading the diaries of a stranger to see if they had any literary interest, but was involved in a more danger- ous enterprise. Now I cannot get away from that adolescent that was—and is—myself. How silly he is, and how sharp;

how early the twig was bent into the worldly posture; how powerfully, when I thought myself alone, was I the subject of influences and policies on the part of others; how little have I later achieved, except the damning diary. What has it all amounted to, these forty-five years since I wrote in my bedroom at The Bower as now I write in my bedroom here in London? My "career"—the work and interest—yes; the achievement I count for little. Only love in one form or another, social exhilaration, solitary walks, and a few books, have left traces. Everything else has slipped between my fingers. As for God, I lived without Him all my youth, and was I better or worse for that?

October 18, 1968
I don't know what has got into me this morning. I am itching with old grudges and angry retorts which I didn't make at the time. They got under my skin like splinters and have stayed there, only coming out later. Perhaps this mood has been brought on by reading Tolstoy's life, that cantankerous old monster. I am beginning to be bored and overpowered by Tolstoy—there is so much of him.

Walked in Regent's Park with Sylvia. Ducks and dahlias, roses not yet bitten by the frost, and in the upper canal discovered the hide-out of the black swans. Lunched with Arnold Smith. Our professional interests differ: he wants to keep the Africans in the Commonwealth; I am interested in relations between Canada and Britain. But I like him personally very much.

October 20, 1968
Donald Mallett to lunch—a friend, perhaps the last of them for me. Went afterwards to the Balthus pictures at the Tate—the claustrophobia of adolescent afternoons, young girls enclosed in curtained rooms singly and in pairs, all slouched in chairs day-dreaming mindlessly, erotically; a Paris street scene that I would buy if I could.

Splendid reviews in the American papers of *Eva Trout*. I am so delighted from every point of view. Also, having been, in these "unfashionable" years for [Elizabeth] as a novelist, always a continuing believer in her genius, I feel such satisfaction at this chorus of praise.

Young Roger Rowley staying in the house. He, Eliza, and Peter Elliston for dinner last night. A bizarre evening for me, as I had just been soaked in the early diaries in which Peter played the central part. "What," I said to him, "have we two to show for our lives, not in terms of 'success' or 'failure', but in living?" "Nothing, nothing at all," Peter said in his new dry voice of realism. Yet the next moment he was off on a fantastic saga of embroidered invention just as rococo as his youthful extravaganzas.

October 27, 1968
The day of protest marches through London. Demonstration against the U.S. Embassy next door expected. I can hear somewhere in the near distance the sounds of horses' hooves—that must be the mounted police. U.S. Marines are installed in the Embassy and closed-circuit TV is on the roof. What is this protest march protesting against? Everything. And what does everything mean? I am as out of touch with this protest as if I lived on another planet. And the young whom I happen to know seem to understand it as little as I do. Sexual freedom, social freedom, outrageous clothes, long hair—if they want these I am all in favour. I also sympathize with the fun of protesting, but the social and political meaning of the "permanent revolution" is gibberish to me. A protest against this permissive society—isn't it punching a pillow?

Roger leaves today. I shall be sorry to see him go, which is more than I can say for some of my guests. He makes me laugh and he is attractive. Moreover, he has a lot of sense.

Do I envy these young men? Not really. Those decisions

and indecisions affecting one's whole future loom so large, and what the family expects of one, what one's contemporaries think of one, how to get hold of a girl, or how to find a job. It's agony shot through with high spirits.

November 12, 1968
I saw Eliza riding in the park yesterday morning, trotting along on a grey nag with her red hair flying in the wind. She wants to buy a stallion from Zsa Zsa Gabor to save it from being gelded.

In the Communications Centre the cypher clerks are onto me about tax-free cigarettes and drink. It is outrageous that they can't have them. Why shouldn't they get some droppings from the diplomat's table? Why the bloody hell can't they? They work as hard as, or harder than, anyone, and everything depends on them and no one pays the least attention to them.

The Lord Mayor's dinner at the Guildhall. Technicolor brilliance of robes and uniforms under the klieg lights, especially the Archbishop's violently purple robes. What an old stage-stealer he is. The Prime Minister [Harold Wilson] standing no nonsense from the City in his speech, which was coldly received. How they hate him! Then a series of drippingly mellifluous exchanges from the Lord Mayor, the Archbishop, the ex-Lord Mayor—reciprocal compliments, jokes, tributes, resounding affirmations of Faith in Youth, sound as ever to the core but with a few rotten spots; the Commonwealth (these tributes sound hollower each year); Britain (hopefully); and the City of London and all that it stands for.

November 15, 1968
In the afternoon dedicated a plaque at the veterans' Star and Garter Home at Richmond, in the company of the United States Ambassador. Made a short and "stirring" speech.

In the evening chaired a big dinner at the Canadian Club. Wore a bloody silly chain and medallion round my neck like a Mayor. Made a fulsome speech introducing Earl McLaughlin—quite disgusted myself.

That woman whom I met at the reception the other day—did I say too much to her? I thought I saw the small-town tightening of the lips, that remorseless glint of satisfaction at having heard scandal and intending to retain and retail it. A walk in Regent's Park, seagulls in sunlight, last roses, copper beeches, swinging my umbrella, exhilaration.

Stout men in Homburgs and double-breasted overcoats walking in pairs and discussing how to beat the new government financial regulations.

A lady came for a drink and began, "It means so much that there is still graciousness to be found in the world." We asked where. "At Claridge's, where I am staying. The flowers in my room, the exquisite manners of the waiters."

December 1, 1968
I like making love as much, if not more, than anything. What else do I like as much, or nearly as much? In some earlier diary I write that what I liked most was the kind of conversation in which characters and motives were dissected. That now seems to me trivial. I do like walking alone in public parks—St. James's Park; Bois de Boulogne; Central Park, New York; Point Pleasant Park, Halifax, Nova Scotia; Christ Church Meadow; Magdalen Park, Oxford; Sud-Park, Köln; the Luxembourg Gardens, Paris; Dumbarton Oaks park, Washington, D.C.; along the canal in Ottawa; round the poop-deck overlooking the Ottawa River; along the Rhine-side walk at Bonn. I like sinking into a movie after a good lunch. Reading would once have come first on my list— I still can't imagine life without it; looking at pictures—yes, in a responsive mood. The transient glow of hospitality given. Some seaports I like, and a town hotel or country house

which is unfamiliar. Smoked salmon and hot baths. I don't know if I *like* drinking but I have to, and I like the effects—sometimes. Smoking is another *must* and only rarely a pleasure. Are addictions different from pleasures?

Things I hate most—flying, or preparing a speech, or reflecting on my own unworthiness.

Lunched at the Travellers with my old friend Tony Payne, now Rector of Lichfield. He arrived in a period shovel hat which would sell well in the King's Road. We had a very good lunch—whisky, then chops and Club claret and Stilton. Tony is in a Retreat in Great College Street for a week. I asked him, "Can you smoke there?" He said, "Yes, on the roof." "Would I like it?" "I don't know how much of a man of God you are." Hard question to answer. Tony and I parted in a glow of friendship.

December 13, 1968

All-day sessions of the Anglo-Canadian Continuing Committee on Trade and Economic Relations. I was in the Chair and listened, understanding a little here and there. Lunch for thirty men here at the house. Cocktails given by the RCMP for the Intelligence Wallahs. One of the English Intelligence people had had dealings with Norman Robertson over cases of people being blackmailed, etc., by the other side. He said that Norman's wisdom and compassion were those of a saint.

January 3, 1969

Waiting for Trudeau. Message telephoned anonymously—"He will not leave the airport alive." So, we start the drama with melodrama; so, I am off to the airport.

January 5, 1969

First meeting between Trudeau and Harold Wilson. The conversation started on NATO. There was a good and full discussion which I do not record as I make it a rule not to include accounts of confidential political and diplomatic negotiations in this diary.

Trudeau said that he was impressed by Wilson's apparently relaxed mood, by his taking time for random conversation. He added that Wilson was a fully political animal as he, Trudeau, was not. He said he would never spend a whole weekend, as Wilson does, talking politics and getting officials around him and going over with them all the speeches he would later make at the Commonwealth Conference. Trudeau was impressed by Wilson's intelligence and dialectical skills. I think that Wilson and Trudeau enjoyed each other and got on perhaps better than Mike and Wilson.

January 23, 1969
Scattered impressions of Trudeau's visit. The press have concentrated quite largely on his "love life". He attacked them for this at his press conference, but he is himself largely responsible. He trails his coat, he goes to conspicuous places with conspicuous women. If he really wants an affair, he could easily manage it discreetly. This is a kind of double bluff.

I lunched on gammon at the Travellers' club and afterwards read a pornographic book in the library. It is the most beautiful room in London. We used not to have any sex in the club library but now it is everywhere, like petrol fumes in the air.

I believe that this notion of the younger generation—embattled and different from any other—may turn out to be a huge hoax. It is certainly a huge bore.

January 24, 1969
Went down in the train from Charing Cross to Hythe for the day. There was Elizabeth waiting at the Central Station, Folkestone. God! how will it be if I must outlive her. We walked on the lees at Folkestone in the mild spring weather under the groin of the cliffs and went back to her house,

Carbery, for dinner. She showed me the outline of her new book, *Pictures and Conversation*. Yesterday was the London birth day of *Eva Trout* and the reviews are just beginning to come out, and already she is at work on the new book. In it she asks the question "Is writing allied to witchcraft?" We drank a lot of 1949 Burgundy and I waited in the dark night, Burgundy-filled, at the little Sandling Station for the London train to come in.

January 25, 1969
A fully spring day of early sunshine in which Sylvia and I walked cheerfully together. I came back and read an old memoir of the fate of my great-great-aunt Catherine, a beautiful, high-spirited girl given to too much novel-reading, who was driven mad by her family and by an overdose of laudanum and thought she was being dragged over broken bottles. She died young and insane.

Matthew Smith says that at my reception at Canada House, to which Trudeau came so reluctantly, Trudeau attacked him for wearing a dinner jacket and told him that he ought to be out in the street joining with the other demonstrators instead of swanning around at a social occasion.

January 27, 1969
I heard Sylvia saying to Bruna, our "wonderful maid", "Mr. Ritchie does not like bacon or fried egg for breakfast." Poor Bruna—she goes into the hospital tomorrow to have a cyst or cancer removed from her breast. Think of her on these black London mornings, getting my Goddamned fried egg ready, toting it up in the lift, toting it—untouched—down again, taking the dog round the block in the dank morning air, and all the time worrying, worrying, "Will they remove my breast?"

Lunch and dinner for Cardinal, the President of the Quebec Council; elaborate food and lousy speeches, but none so bad as that of Whitlock, the Under-Secretary of State for

Foreign Affairs, who quoted Rupert Brooke—"Some corner of a foreign field that is for ever England"—and spoke of World War graves to this group of Quebecers who regard those wars as British imperialists' ventures in which their countrymen were used as cannon fodder.

February 5, 1969
Recovering from flu and from the jungle of high fever, restless turning in the "burrows of the nightmare". In that fetid region all the paper mottoes of faith and conduct are swept out of touch and sight.

I spent the afternoon recovering in bed. Read *Antony and Cleopatra* and became so moved and inflamed by it that I could not get to sleep at night.

February 10, 1969
Back from Stansted. The two days there were extraordinarily happy and healthy. I was exhilarated to wake up to the famous parkscape from my bedroom, the "rides" through the forest, the black trees with a snowy foreground and the sky cold and cloudless with visibility to infinity, infinity all enclosed in the woods and avenues of Stansted. The familiar enchantment of the place operated once again. Everything pleased. Driving round the estate with Eric in his new Land Rover, watching the pigeons rise from a field of kale, watching Mary paint flower pictures in her attic studio, and standing in the library before a fire of great logs, turning over photograph albums.

March 1, 1969
Eliza has come to stay. She and I walk round the Square in a mild thaw from a small snowfall, two tall figures nodding heads, a rustle of talk, plans, contrivances, phrases for dealing with dilemmas, rattles round as we mimic communication together.

Young Marshall from Ottawa came to see me about the

visit of the Canadian Parliamentary Committee, with the suggestion that all their briefings here should be tape-recorded and attended by the press. Of course this means that no one will speak frankly. All this is in the name of "participation", to build up parliamentary committees so that they feel they are participating in the formulation of policy, that all options, including neutrality, have been considered and all voices heard. I am divided about all this; I see what Trudeau is driving at. He is impressed by the alienation of people from their government and their feeling that foreign and defence policies are formulated mysteriously and imposed on them. He is indeed undertaking to change the system of Cabinet solidarity and the organization of Executive and Legislature; "broaden the base", and also secure a new kind of "General Will", incarnate in himself. He may be right in his diagnosis of the gravity of the social disease. As to the cure, he is looking for it by an apparently endless process of review, of digging institutions up by the roots to examine them, of shaking up Establishment figures. And then what? He is not really a revolutionary. Is this process aimed at the reversal of alliances or at real economic and social programs of change? No. Is it just a grandiose and perhaps necessary manoeuvre to establish communication? How much of it is done with mirrors? Well, I am with him so far, but is he with me? I think he believes that diplomats as a class are an organized lobby against change. Perhaps he is right—especially elderly diplomats.

Met horrible literary female, and felt a shuddering repugnance for this malicious, round-heeled, blowsy *bore*.

March 16, 1969

Two and a half more years, with luck, of living on a millionaire's income in a London mansion of the kind that disappeared from ordinary life thirty years ago, with five servants, a chauffeur and the biggest car in London, with whisky and cigarettes virtually free—and presto! down we go to a heavily taxed middle-class income; from invitations to Buckingham Palace and Chatsworth to the company of a few old friends, if any left after absence of years; from being surrounded by the young, who find it convenient to lodge here, to seeing only contemporaries; from a diversity of company to relative isolation; from influence and inside information to neither of either. On top of all this—old age, impotence, loss of hair and memory!

March 23, 1969

I am having my portrait painted. An artist—even a bad artist—can create mayhem around him. I have a craving to destroy the portrait—and perhaps to destroy the painter.

Eliza plays her scales over in the long drawing-room in the half-light of this grey Sunday afternoon. She props her music against the Barbara Hepworth bronze. Facing her is the ill-fated portrait, still on its easel. The floor is strewn with the matting on which he stood while painting. When the artist departs, the room will revert to its parlour-like sterility. Yesterday Eliza and I went to Chiswick. The sun came out and went in again. There were colonies of purple and yellow crocuses on the lawns. We went into the house and stood in a window embrasure of an empty, unfurnished little panelled room, looking out together at the cypresses and urns and obelisks and allées. Then we went to Chiswick Mall by the river and watched blue-sailed boats scudding before the March wind, and chose a house in which to live called Strawberry House—Georgian, with a vine-clad balcony overlooking the river.

April 15, 1969

Walking through St. James's Park I encountered that gypsy woman whom I have seen telling people's fortunes. I decided to try mine. She took my hand, looked at it, and instantly said, "They will never make a gentleman out of you." I can remember nothing else in the fortune.

I had a long talk with Jerry Hardy about politics. The truth is that he and I know that there is no interest in Canada in tightening relations with the United Kingdom or in reporting home on British policies. Dispatches from Paris are read because French politics affect our future as a nation, whereas Britain has virtually no influence at all. The "British connection" seems to be receding out of view. Only the Crown remains.

In the evening went to a crowded cocktail party and accidentally stepped on my hostess's toe. She gave a real squeak of anguish.

April 17, 1969

They are going to make me a Companion of Canada, so now I am a registered member, in good standing, of the Canadian Establishment. I was going to write that my mother would have been pleased, if she had been alive, but I don't think she would have understood what it was all about. The only awards she respected were "real" British awards.

McMillan, the president of the C.N.R., came to lunch He is a Winnipeg Westerner and spoke of the revolt of the West against the Trudeau regime, saying that in the Party caucuses in the West there is a strong underground movement of Western separatism.

More Westerners in the afternoon, including an oil-business couple. I took very much to her but not so much to him. There was an air of over-used charm about him and he smelt of hair essence or after-shave cream or something, and kept referring to Canadians as "Canucks". Perhaps he is an American.

April 20, 1969

Woke feeling levitated, put on my blue pullover, taxied to Regent's Park, walked happily with my head full of projects in the spring sunshine by the rock garden, to and fro over the bridges; looked at some nesting coots; saw three nuns quacking away together on a bench; knew that I had not too long to live; remembered that day Elizabeth and I walked down the road by the Park lined with flowering cherry trees. It was during the war, and I was recovering from flu and it was my first day out. It must have been the same time in April as today, because the fruit trees lining the road were just in bloom.

Went down to lunch at Knebworth with the Cobbolds, charming elderly couple (about my age). They garden together, clear out the undergrowth in the "wilderness", making do with one gardener where once there were sixteen. (The gardens of England's Stately Homes before the Fall must have been the most over-staffed organizations in history.) The Cobbolds have three upstanding, nice-mannered, intelligent sons, and the appropriate quota of grandchildren. Lord Cobbold is a former Director of the Bank of England, now Lord Chamberlain. Has a grace-and-favour house in St. James's Palace overlooking the courtyard. Knebworth, built by Bulwer Lytton—or rebuilt by him—is a German romantic fantasy of the 1840s, unfortunately tidied up by Lady Cobbold's uncle, Lutyens, who was appalled by the gimcrackery, which is the only point of the house, and wanted to uncover and restore the original uninteresting fourteenth-century house. Now the remaining nineteenth-century heraldic figures, gargoyles, and Victorian armorial bits and pieces are quite literally falling off the exterior. Warnings out everywhere—"Beware of falling stone-work". We had excellent roast beef for lunch.

May 12, 1969
In the morning went to a NATO commemorative service in the new Guards Chapel built to replace the one destroyed in the blitz. I was revolted by the sermon from a sanctimonious old Dogan plastering over this necessary military alliance with pseudo-Christian pi-jaw.

In the afternoon, as an escape from an east-windy grey day in Oxford Street I popped into a German film entitled *Sex and Love*. It was the kind of thing to give pornography a bad name. I came away fearing that I might have been put off sex for life.

The French Embassy party in the evening ostensibly given for the Finnish Ambassador and his wife, but nobody spoke to them and they looked like Finns out of water.

May 18, 1969
Went down on the train to Devon with Derick Amory, former Chancellor of the Exchequer, former High Commissioner to Ottawa, and could, I believe—if he had wanted to—have been Prime Minister. I am becoming very fond of him. He is ironical, invalidish (terrible wounds from the First War, served again in the Second), now a Director of the Hudson's Bay Company. He lives by faith or stoicism, covering permanent pain. In dealing with people he pushes away all directness with kind inquiries and malicious asides. He spends his week-ends with his old aunt (eighty-eight) in her bungalow in the grounds of her Tudor former house. We stayed there for the night. Derick's aunt is a redoubtable old Anglo-Irish woman, lost a husband and a brother in the First War and all her three sons in the Second War, now shrivelled, shrunken, wearing an old felt hat and gardening boots as she stumped into the yard to greet us. But in three minutes her recalcitrance, quick-wittedness, and engagingness were apparent. Round the garden we went with her. She was fond of this flower, disparaging about that flower, asking no questions, giving no answers, occasionally a crooked smile—and she had us!

May 20, 1969
To the Mounties' Musical Ride at the Devon Agricultural Show. Many bulls, cows, goats, sheep, in procession before

the Mounties got a look-in. Presented prizes, took the salute (slight uncertainty on my part as to when to take off my hat and when to put it back on again), toured the tents, tasted local cheese, drank local small cider. Most tricky was my visit to the "Lines" of the Mounties. I patted horses' necks, started talking to each member of the Mounties' team, began to run down on matey chat, knew they knew it, felt a fool. Suppose they only saw a silly old man—what does it matter?

May 22, 1969
Macdonald, President of the Privy Council, and Mrs. Macdonald are here on a visit from Ottawa. We gave a luncheon for them today. He has the reputation of being one of the most "with it" Ministers, close to the Prime Minister and opposed to the old establishment. One of his staff warned me that Mrs. Macdonald is strongly anti-English. But in spite of my "Englishness" I got on very well with her. She is an extremely attractive woman, tall, fair, fresh-skinned, and her talk has freshness too. She is, however, imbued with the anti-External Affairs virus.

June 5, 1969
Yet another Cabinet Minister—Pepin, the Minister of Trade and Commerce. Went to the airport to meet him. I had never seen him before but guessed as he came off the plane that he would be carrying a spare suit on a hook under a cellophane cover, and I was right. He is big and jovial, and looks a cross between an Assyrian emperor and Groucho Marx. Very easy and open in manner. A group of us went back to the Dorchester to work on his speech. It is a long time since I have put in such a session, yet how many hundreds of times I have done it and with so many different Ministers—battles of wits, will, prestige, over the inclusion of one civil servant's draft or the substitution for it of another; attempts by civil servants, gently, firmly, persistently, to eliminate the Minis-

ter's wilder, bolder—or just more vote-getting—passages in the text. Block that metaphor! Drop that joke! A final exhausted tug-of-war over the elimination of the word "despite" in paragraph 4.

Home, and a quick change, and to Anne Fleming's party. Literary figures, a don or two, and Andrew Devonshire. Our hostess, Anne, looks sadder and more human since her husband Ian Fleming's death. Diana Cooper, in a pyjama suit, greeted me in joke tones of thrilling sincerity. In the next room Elizabeth and Stuart Hampshire stood murmuring by the bar. The writer Leslie Hartley sat on a sofa like a giant panda, being patted and petted, making mumbling and inconclusive sounds. He is loved by all. Our hostess, in grey and diamonds, was alternately pert and pensive. Of herself she said, "In my youth I did what I wanted and never knew guilt. Women's frustrations are different and simpler than those of men, and come from not getting what they want, usually something quite uncomplicated—a husband, a lover, a home, children—but men suffer from not knowing what or whom they want."

June 14, 1969
Went to a stupid reception at the Dorchester given by the Sheik of Abu Dhabi. It was full of hawk-nosed sons of the desert with lustrous eyes, and oil men, and Foreign Office Middle East experts who would like to be oil men. When I was presented to the Sheik he said, condescendingly, "We have heard of your country and its good reputation."

Dinner with Elizabeth. She thinks that one is born with "innate ideas", reflections of the social and mental climate of one's parents. If this is so, in my own case the idea of loyalty (and its obverse, disloyalty) was a dominant. Loyalty, but not necessarily fidelity. She thinks that instead of being awarded the Order of Canada I should have been knighted. I explained that this was impossible for a Canadian, and that in any case I did not want a knighthood. I should feel a damn fool among my friends at home, being addressed as "Sir Charles". In fact I am very pleased to have this award. After all, I have acted for my client, Canada, for thirty-five years and defended its interests like a son of the law and swallowed my own prejudices in the process.

September 27, 1969
A muggy, murky, misanthropic day. Went to the doctor about my itching legs. He has always been such a sensible, reassuring practitioner, but I believe that he has now gone mad. He had a speck of froth on his lips and his kind horse face looked blurred. Without ado upon my entry he asked, "Shall I read you some of my poems?" Then one poem followed another, sunsets, leaves turning... "You see, I paint in words." And then, odder and more personal ones, one called "The Midnight Doctor of Hythe". "Why Hythe?" he asked on a puzzled note. He is in fact Elizabeth's doctor also. In his dream he is driving around the sleeping town in his Mini thinking of those lying awake in their beds tortured by anxiety, on whose heads he might lay a calming hand. Later in the day he telephoned me to ask my advice about a letter he is writing to *The Times* which he believes "will bring the Government down".

On my way back from the doctor's I sat in a deck-chair in the park and must have dropped my wallet, which unfortunately had £40 in it.

October 4, 1969
I went to Oxford to my old college for the annual dinner of the Pembroke Society. After dinner when the very old and the young had gone to bed, my sixty-odd-year-old surviving contemporaries got together at one of the tables in Hall and the serious drinking began, a new bottle of whisky being ordered every five minutes. I would not have recognized any

of them if I had fallen over them in a London street, but in that Hall, where we had all sat together drinking when young, their faces gradually got attached to earlier faces once belonging to them, and we peered and stared at each other through the mists of time and whisky.

On the morning after, I pensively promenaded the meadows and lanes and quads of grey, autumnal, out-of-term Oxford, encountering by the way several of last night's convivial contemporaries. We passed each other with averted eyes, nursing our separate hangovers.

October 5, 1969
Earlier in the day I had lunch with an old painter. He tells me that some young women are "gerontophiles", meaning that they prefer old men. He says he has a list and offered to lend it to me. At lunch there was a woman who said, "I know my husband is an old lecher but there are so many pansies about that I prefer him like that."

The afternoon was depressing. I had to read to the "Canada-based staff" the Minister's telegram about the withdrawals of personnel and the new economies. I thought it best not to try the Pollyanna note but to give them the treatment direct. I was upset by the whole proceeding because of the botched and clumsy way it is being done under this absurdly poised time gun and for the wrong reasons— almost non-existent economies—when it could and should have been done over a period of time as a process of reorganization and a re-targeting of the functions of the Department. The present exercise is being conducted in a cloud of public and political criticism of the Department. It seems almost punitive and gives our people to think that their work has all been a waste of time and that the Department would like to shuffle them off anywhere to get them off the pay-roll. Louis Rogers says that my morale is bad.

Ted Heath said to me the other day, "You Canadians have a good Foreign Service; why are you buggering it about?"

November 24, 1969
Lunched with a group of super-rich oil men at the Dorchester, organized by Roy Thomson,* who said it did him good to hear talk which seldom got below the level of a billion dollars. I found the conversation fascinating, though sometimes incomprehensible. Plainly I had been invited as a social or symbolic gesture—I came with the flowers, the smoked salmon, and the wine, to show that the old pirate knew the amenities.

I am not at my ease with tycoons, except, for some reason, Jewish ones.

In the office we spend two-thirds of our time administering ourselves and coping with the swarm of regulations that our new "management approach" has resulted in. Questionnaires, union contracts, program budgeting, task forces, goals targets, ratings, policy analysis, computerized forecasts. There is no policy work in the office, and Louis Rogers and I are both bored.

December 4, 1969
I was thinking back today to my October visit to Ottawa, Trudeau's capital and court, ruled by an icy enigma. He seems to have cowed Parliament, the Civil Service, and his Cabinet colleagues. He does not bully—his method is more oblique, a mixture of chilly scorn and scorching impatience, and all overlaid with the quick, disarming smile.

How well does he govern Canada? He has been quick to see the need to hold and weld into political society the young and the outsiders. He has attacked and is demolishing the

*Lord Thomson of Fleet; Canadian newspaper owner.

obsolete assumptions behind the criminal code. His rule is
only at its outset. He has joined battles but not yet won them.
Will his method work in Canada, a country traditionally
governed by compromise, by subterfuge, all wrapped up in
the opaque jargon of politicians who learned their style from
Mackenzie King? Will Canadians long endure Trudeau's
explicitness of will and his caustic language? Could these
begin to goad and irritate? Behind this question lies the limit
of his power and his quest to extend it. Some say that this
quest for power will lead him to an American or Gaullist
conception of the Executive; that he plans by stages to bring
not only the Civil Service but Parliament itself to heel. Yet he
is a cautious man—he shows more than he moves. First there
is a resounding defiance of established policy and patterns;
then prudent pragmatic withdrawal, with still some ground
gained; then a sally in another direction. So in the end he is
compelled, like every Canadian Prime Minister before him,
to a balancing act—to enrage one section of the population
one day, to appease them the next, to play one region or
interest or prejudice or race against another. This he does with
virtuoso effect.

Is Trudeau a surgical analyst come in to cut off the
layers of inefficiency and out-of-date ideas? Can he construct
something solid in the place of what he wants to change?
Again a question. Every statement about Trudeau crumbles
into its contradiction. An intellectual, yes, but *is* he? If so, his
conversation does not reveal one. A social swinger, yes, yet
not at ease socially. A power-loving French-Canadian politician, but how different in tone and temper from any of that
breed. What then has one got to go on? He is a dandy, an
actor, a loner, a secret—even a shy—man.

He dominates the Canadian scene without a rival. The
Opposition, at any rate the Conservative Opposition, is feeble
and sterile. This is how things look in December 1969—how
will they look two years from now? The going will get tough

for Trudeau. He could end up as an exploded myth. His problem will be not only to establish "mastery" but to produce radical solutions to match his radical criticisms. Or he could turn out to be a sphinx without a secret.

As to the international scene, they say that Trudeau would like it to get up and walk away. Also, he is reacting against what he thinks to be the over-responsiveness, busy-body-ism, do-good-ism, of his predecessors, and hence to their instrument, the Department of External Affairs. There is animus in his reaction. He would like not so much to destroy the Department as to serve it a very sharp lesson. What is that lesson? Part of it is simply to come to heel. But there is more to it than that. He has genuinely concluded that our operation is over-extended, wrongly targeted, and out of date. Just as he has set up a task force on the role of the soldier, so he wants a categorical answer to the question no one has ever satisfactorily answered—What is the role of the diplomat? The answer he would like would be a cybernetic answer, a computer answer, something that could be shown on a graph, an extrapolation, something fished out of a "think tank", for he has a weakness for this language and these concepts. What he does not want is an answer from the Department which implies a mystique, a trade secret, something elect, inherited from Trudeau's predecessors and shared between them. He has a right to put the questions, but not to the animus with which he puts them. It is true that there has crept into the Foreign Service a note of both self-congratulation and self-pity which irritates others besides the Prime Minister. It is true that a portion of the work done by the Service is not focussed on concrete Canadian interests, that telegrams assiduously and conscientiously prepared sink into the Department without a trace, without response or influence. This unreality is partly a function of size. At the insistence of the politicians we have opened many missions which are far from essential, and at our own instigation we have over-padded many of our missions abroad. It is time that we and all the other Departments functioning abroad took a look at our operations and expenditures.

December 11, 1969

To see Burke Trend* at the Cabinet Office. He says, and I think so too, that the great task that faces our political leaders is to humanize the computer age, to give back to people a sense of connection with the growing scale and impersonality of modern technology. He wants Wilson and Trudeau to talk about this when next they meet. Certainly Trudeau is one of the few politicians to be impressed with this question of the dehumanization of our life and environment, which is really behind so many of the protest movements of our times.

Went to the Beefsteak Club and was richly rewarded as Harold Macmillan† was there in wonderful form; witty, wise, wide-ranging talk.

Margaret Meagher is staying with us. She is very good value, down-to-earth in a Nova Scotian way.

Bobby Rae,‡ now a Rhodes Scholar at Balliol, came to lunch. Intelligent, left-wing views, student power at Toronto University. Dislikes Trudeau as being much too conservative.

December 12, 1969—Manchester

Having got drunkish the night before, I had to rise at 6:30 on a pitch-black morning, pile into my clothes, and set off with Sylvia by train for my visit to Manchester. On the train they gave us a huge breakfast—sausages, bacon and eggs, God knows what—I couldn't touch it. I wondered how I would get through the day, though in fact got through it very well. There is nothing like being treated as Royalty, and being gracious back, to bolster morale, and one sees how those in

---

*Sir Burke Trend, Secretary of the Cabinet.
†Rt. Hon. Harold Macmillan, British Prime Minister 1957-1963.
‡Bob Rae is currently leader of the Ontario New Democratic Party.

the public eye go on and on forever and never lose the taste for it. Manchester lived up to its reputation for murk. On arrival we were escorted down the platform by the station-master and Rolls-Royced to the Manchester Liners' new building which I was to open. I was met at the door by Stoker, the Chairman of the Company. Then I swung a bottle of champagne (which to my surprise broke, as it should have done, on the first shot) to launch the new building. Then unveiled a totem-pole, then shook hands with two hundred people, then, after a very long lunch in a very hot room, speeches by Stoker and myself, both attempting to be facetious. He is a "whirlwind of energy", with a nice Scotch wife and a son who wants to be an artist. He presides over a container shipping line, and all the talk was of the container trade from Manchester to Montreal. I found this interesting and instructive. The container business is progressively eliminating dockers—another example of making people unnecessary. No more dockers, no more porters. Why not no more diplomats? How our Prime Minister would love to computerize the whole Foreign Service and eliminate the human element. After lunch we all bundled into buses and drove, in the driving rain, along the ship canal to see the containers being lowered into the ships. Later Sylvia and I went to stay with the Lord Mayor and Lady Mayoress for the night in the Town Hall in which the Mayor resides. It must be one of the most stupendous buildings of the Victorian age, built at the peak of Manchester's greatness. The State Apartments were vast, gloomy, decorated, painted, tiled, panelled, frescoed; there were outsize stone and marble staircases and ironwork everywhere. The Mayor and Mayoress gave a dinner party of the local magnates for us. The Manchester people are very forthcoming and not at all gentlemanly—what a relief!

The next day we set out after breakfast in the Mayorial Rolls for a tour of the city. It was raining, with drifting fog patches which mercifully obscured some of the new housing units, great grey blocks of prefabricated flats, sited in a sea of mud. By contrast the little old (Industrial Revolution) bleak hutments with outdoor plumbing looked almost cozy. They are hauling Manchester out of the nineteenth century at a great rate and building, building, everywhere, as they are in the vast industrial sprawl through which we passed in the train on our way home to London, giving one a notion of the huge industrial wealth and strength of this country. And everywhere new housing, high-rises, and terraces in former fields.

December 16, 1969
Kenneth Clark in *Civilisation*, discussing Turner's use of colour, writes: "Colour was considered immoral, perhaps rightly because there is an immediate sensation which makes its effect independently of those ordered memories which are the basis of morality."

Since I was eleven years old, perhaps before, I have at intervals played a kind of game in which I opened my eyes, looked about me, and willed myself to blot out all except what I at that moment saw before me, pretending that all was completely new, seen for the first time. So, too, with people. I have looked at my loved ones with an eye, and listened to them with an ear, from the outside. I have had at such times a sense of moral irresponsibility, a sort of self-induced drugged state, intensification of vision, dissociation from the human element. This game is dangerous. It has sometimes led to words and actions which would never have been in the linear order of my behaviour. These "fresh beginnings" have in fact not been beginnings, but escapes from habitual behaviour. They are a form of aesthetic immoralism, often bringing later remorse, but highly delightful at the time.

Diana erupted into Wilton's today to join me for lunch wearing trousers and a-yachting cap with "H.M.S. *Indomitable*" on it. She was in a gale of spirits from having parked her car with all four wheels on the pavement after banging into a van. She is not only accident-prone, I believe she revels in accidents and risks. She is, now nearing eighty, a woman for all ages, equally enchanting to that ninety-year-old billionaire Paul Getty, to up-and-coming politicians, to writers and artists, waiters and policemen, to philandering skirt-chasers, homosexuals and lesbians. Yet this Pied Piper plays no soothing or well-worn airs; she is unexpected, fresh as a clever child, has kept her immaculate beauty and wears the lost glamour of pre-1914 with a touch of slapstick. She enjoys the company of the rich, but hasn't forgotten what it is to be hard up. She tried to save me money on the luncheon by insisting on one lobster cutlet only between us, but Mr. Marx, the proprietor, circumvented her and managed to charge me £10.

February 15, 1970
Week-end at Hythe. Cold, sunny weather, but quite warm when you had been walking briskly up and down the sea-front past the Victorian sea-side lodgings, past the 1920 bungalows (one of which is the sea-side house in *The Death of the Heart*). Sun on calm blue water, a few stoutly coated figures fishing at the water's edge, passing dog-walkers all muffled up. The curve of the bay, Dungeness in the distance, and behind me the romantic view of Hythe topped by its church tower. Then walking back past the now leafless trees of Lady's Walk (which are in dripping leaf when Karen and her lover walk there in *The House in Paris**), and so on up the hill to Carbery. Elizabeth does not join me in my walks. She says that neither of us ever stops talking and that when she talks as she walks the cold air catches in her throat and makes her cough. Her mind is now fixed on Ireland, going to live there. She says she will prowl around a little Regency terrace at Clontarf and choose a house there, or somewhere like it,

*Published in 1935.

not too far from Dublin. She will stay at Hythe only as long as I stay in London.

March 10, 1970

Lunched today at the Carlton Club with a Conservative peeress. She and I are not made for each other. She kept asking me questions like "Is it compulsory in Canada for every individual to *destroy* any waste paper in his possession?" I said, "No, I don't think so. Probably most people just chuck it out." "But I am assured, on very good authority, that it *is* compulsory in Canada." (Well, if she knows, why the hell ask me?)

As I was lapping up my machine-made turtle soup my nose began to spout blood, drops falling on the virgin snow of the tablecloth. I bolted off past the tables of Conservative MPs to the Gents', and tried to ice my nose. When I returned to the table, the peeress said, in a brisk voice, "That shows you have been overdoing things."

April 22, 1970

Particles of the past disturb my vision of today. I cannot throw away the scratched gramophone record of my particular experience. The needle is stuck in the groove and plays the same old tunes. Never more so than during this visit to Mary in the beamed and raftered cottage that she has left me in her will. She is one who "lives in the past". That sounds to be a dreary occupation. I am not so sure that it is. In these last years when she has lived alone a loveless life of small friendships and village squabbles, she has gone over and over the past with such absorption that it has become far more real and vivid than the daily jogtrot. However, her version of the years which we shared is wildly different from my own. Which of us is lying? Perhaps neither. So much for history. Certainly I do not come well out of her story. (Elizabeth once said, "There is no woman who can't knock a man off his perch if she tries hard enough.") Yet as she and I sat side by side on a slatted wooden bench in her sunny garden, it seemed we were two old people turning over pages in a book we had written together. Who else but we two knew of this or that? "Is the smell of melting tar on a road still your favourite scent, Mary, as you said that day when we walked back from the beach house? And what about Mrs. Pulsifer in the seaside lodging, calling upstairs, 'Breakfast is ready, bar frying the bacon.' " Now Mary says she loves her dog more than any man or woman.

May 8, 1970
For more than a week this hot, fine, flawless weather has gone on. I spend hours of each day in the parks, among the strollers and the lovers (two are making love in a group of daffodils!). The sun is drawing out the scent of the wallflowers. The burnished cavalry of the Household pass slowly down the Mall. Buckingham Palace has been refaced smart for the Queen's return from Australia. The Season is getting under way.

More echoes of the past at Laurence's cocktail party. Laurence himself, whom I remember as a musical stripling, is a puce-faced and portly ex-opera singer. His cousin Marcie (an old flirt of mine) is now a broad-faced peasant with crinkled apple cheeks. There was a florid gentleman in a spotted tie there. I did not identify him, until the moment of departure, with an elegant and dissipated figure who was at Oxford with me and whose circle of "Golden Youths" I envied. We spoke of Billy Coster.* I said, "Billy haunts me." "Me too." But as we talked of him he seemed to recede into a mocking laugh.

October 19, 1970
How much I miss Norman Robertson—how often I wish that I could talk to him. Nobody replaces him for me, or ever will.

* William Bay Coster, an Oxford friend.

Back again to the diary after an immense interval and in a very different climate, for now we live in a climate created by others, those few in Quebec who have, in one of the most extraordinary exploits in our history, held up a nation to ransom.* They have sought out the vulnerable parts in our society and are twisting and twisting the knife in them. Here in London they want to put Canada House under police protection, and also our house. I cannot believe that if I were kidnapped the present government would pay one cent for my ransom. At home it sounds like war but it is not—it is blackmail. Our immense Anglo-Canadian reserves of security—never a revolution, never a civil war, never a defeat, never an enemy occupation, never a humiliation—are at last being drawn upon. Our unbroken national luck has turned, and anger and fear combined may break down our national basis of compromise. Mike Pearson on TV was wise to remind us of this danger. Today a newly arrived French Canadian on the staff said to me, "I am ashamed to be a French Canadian. I feel I should skulk through the streets." I said, "That is complete nonsense. We are all in this together. All Canadians feel the same." But do *all* Canadians? I feel and think insistently about this sombre tragedy.

October 20, 1970
The funeral of M. Laporte. Every time the telephone twitches I expect more bad news from Ottawa. I have spent most of this last week on the long-distance telephone talking to Ed Ritchie† at External Affairs and then relaying messages to and fro between him and Dennis Greenhill at the Foreign Office about the kidnappings. Fortunately one could not have two more sensible and unwordy men to deal with.

---

*On October 5, Jasper Cross, the British Trade Commissioner in Montreal, was kidnapped by the terrorist Front de Libération du Québec. This was followed by the kidnapping and subsequent murder of Pierre Laporte, Deputy Premier of Quebec.
†Under-Secretary of State for External Affairs.

November 1, 1970
Elizabeth is just back from Ireland where she had revisited Bowen's Court* in a busload of Catholic nuns, priests, and acolytes. The house, she says, is gone without a trace; the ground where it stood so smooth that she could only identify the place where the library was by the prunus tree that once used to obscure the light in one of the windows. She says it is better gone than degraded. She is happier, she says, in a different way, now than ever before—the happiness of old age, the day-to-day kind, sensuous pleasure in the visible world. She wants to go on *living*, and so do I.

I suppose Jasper Cross must be dead by now. A small, scruffy collection of Communists were presenting a petition today at the door of the United States Embassy as Elizabeth and I came back from lunch. The other day we had to evacuate MacDonald House because of a bomb scare.

January 31, 1971
Lunched with Ted Heath, now Prime Minister, at Chequers. He was very brisk with his no-nonsense manner and his determined joviality. I like the man because he treats me as a friend, or a friendly acquaintance. Of course I knew him quite well when he was Leader of the Opposition. I feel at ease with him, which I rarely do with Prime Ministers while they are in office. They are usually all right before and after. I certainly never felt at ease with his predecessor, Wilson.

February 1, 1971
I have been re-reading Thackeray's *Pendennis* and recovering from the itch. Pendennis is a young barrister in the 1830s, a man-about-town. After all, *has* London life changed so much since then? Or rather, is the life-style of such young men so very different? *Pendennis* is a sort of English version of Flaubert's *Sentimental Education*. Very acute it is, too.

*Elizabeth Bowen's family home in County Cork.

In the evening went to meet the Quebec Police delegation, who are here for consultation with the British. The head man is a Norman French Canadian, blue-eyed, strawberry colour. Every so often you see that pure Norman type in Canada. He spoke of the FLQ and said that to them separatism was only a jumping-off place. What they really wanted was a revolution against the "Establishment". He spoke as an intelligent policeman, saying that if you read nothing for three months but Che Guevara, Marx, Mao, etc., it would not be at all difficult to think as they do.

After he left, a dreary little party here of middle-aged people talking about Youth. Always the repetition of the same boring sentiments... "I didn't know whether it was a boy or a girl"... "Mind you, I can tolerate long hair provided it is clean"... "They are brought up too soft"... "They despise money but they are always looking for a handout." My trouble is that I can understand the misbehaviour of the younger generation, but not their aspirations.

February 14, 1971
St. Valentine's Day. Went to see Nancy Mitford in hospital where she lies—dying? She says that people always tell her that she would not really have enjoyed living in the reign of Louis XIV because of the horrors of the medical treatments, but that, judging by her medical experience in the last few years, she might just as well have lived in the age of Louis XIV. She tried some jokes and so did I. We drank a little of her champagne. I brought her a bunch of freesias that I got off a barrow at the Marble Arch. I was touched—and surprised—at her being so glad to see me, but felt, as I often do visiting the sick, that I talked too much and nervously, hoping to amuse. Later I walked in the windy park feeling very sad about Nancy and about life.

March 28, 1971
Yesterday was a day of inexplicable exhilaration, of total

happiness. Sylvia and I went down to Woodstock for the night. We arrived in the late afternoon and walked in Blenheim Park. The landscaped lake, the theatrical bridges, the woods behind, were all misted over as though seen through gauze in the ballet *Swan Lake*. It was like walking by the lake in the Bois together when we were first married, and the bedroom up the twisting staircase at the Bear Inn was a kind of bird-cage, like our bedroom in the rue Singer in Paris.

March 29, 1971

I can no more imagine life after retirement than life after death. When I wrote to Ed Ritchie and told him that I did not wish to "cling to this job", I meant precisely the opposite. I *do* wish to cling to this job, and of course he knows that I do.

Elizabeth is in the Hythe Nursing Home. There is a sky above which makes you disbelieve in God—an opaque, inexorable sulk, unchanging, like a mood that is going to last forever.

Douglas LePan comes to see me. He has begun to write poetry again after twenty years of silence. He and I drink together. We are friends.

April 24, 1971

The Duchess of Kent here for a tea party for Dr. Best of insulin fame. The thing about Royalty (which she must have learned after, or just before, entering that enclosed order) is the slow-motion bit—never hurry, just cool it and keep every step, every gesture, every word, limpidly leisurely. It is a game of control. If any of the other actors in the scene get out of phase by word or gesture, control them with the slightest jerk of the reins. It's dressage. No wonder Princess Anne is good at it—she was trained that way. And against this background, conversation of dedicated platitudes; any throwaway line from the Royalty sounds, to the uninitiated, like an indiscretion.

In the afternoon to St. Paul's Cathedral. The Duchess of

Kent says that it would be impossible to be inside that Cathedral without believing in God. I feel exactly the opposite, as if I were in a magnificent, poorly filled opera house.

April 26, 1971
Week-end with the Sitwells. We drove over to Easton Neston. As always there was a wonderful and enjoyable mix of people there coming and going, up and down the grandiose staircase past the statues in their niches and the painted grisailles, in and out of the superb drawing room with its elaborate plaster-work. In all the rooms, seated or semi-recumbent figures lounging, talking, reading, making their entrances and their exits. A house of echoes and reflections—echoes on the stone staircase, on the long parquet-floored gallery, on the paving stones of the hall, reflections from the long windows which frame the formal gardens and the ornamental water. Our hostess, dear Kisty, is a charmer, so clever and so funny and a Scottish naturalness about her.

May 19, 1971
A letter from the Department—"I regretfully must confirm that you should plan your retirement at the normal date, that is, September 23, 1971." So that's that. It will take some sharp hustling to get out of this house by that date, with two months of the London Season and continual entertaining coming in between, and then the dead month of August. It is the end of thirty-seven years in the Foreign Service.

They, particularly Louis Rogers, are trying to get me out of my spacious office in Canada House and into a utilitarian third-floor box in MacDonald House. No—I and my office go together.

June 6, 1971
Walked in Kensington Gardens. I had got up very early—5:30 a.m.—pulled on my pants, old sweater, collected key

and three cigarettes. The park was completely empty. The morning was fine, foreboding heat, the sun just risen. I walked and walked till I came to the statue of Queen Victoria sculpted by her daughter which stands in front of Kensington Palace. Turning round the statue I came under the vine trellis into the garden. After so much green of trees and grass, its yellows and browns and pinks, the red of the tulips and the brown of the wallflowers, burst on my eyes with a delightful shock. I was alone and happy. For some reason I thought of my mother and remembered how she used to challenge us boys to look straight into her eyes and how we tried and always flinched before that potent, mocking, mysterious gaze, something leonine about it, not feline.

June 14, 1971

Itching like hell—I wonder whether this is the change of life.

I am emptied and flattened by the hours of Wagner with Loelia.* The second Act of *Tristan* vented its full power. Never that I can remember have I been so totally transported into a realm of passion and tragedy which was yet quite credible. I feel as if Loelia and I had been consumed and exhausted in the same revelation. I thought of ringing her up and asking her how her Wagner is settling down, but she is at Ascot with her husband. The loss of credibility and the lessening of interest comes in the third Act, with the endless dying of Tristan. Never underestimate Wagner's capacity for stretching a duet. We were in the theatre for six hours.

Earlier in the day I lunched at Aspinall's, the new club in Berkeley Square. All the people who used to go to the West End restaurants have now migrated, either to the new gaming clubs or to Chelsea and Knightsbridge. At the table next to us were a quartet of young bucks—quite a change from the arty Chelsea world. Perhaps with the revival of

*Loelia, Duchess of Westminster, now Hon. Lady Lindsay of Dowhill.

Edwardian women's hats this year will come revival of the Edwardian gamblers and womanizers, the earliest progenitors of Mayfair.

July 12, 1971
Returned to London from a Disraelian week-end in the country at the d'Avigdor-Goldsmids. Gloriously hot weekend; roses, roses all the way. House running on the velvet wheels of the rich. The diversified and diverting company staying in the house included my now-favourite writer, Anthony Powell. What more could one ask? Powell himself is unalarming to an almost alarming degree, young in manner, extremely nice, natural and charming.

July 16, 1971
End of the Season—and what a Season! Lunched with the Queen Mother. On the dining room table great silver bowls of outsize sweet peas breathing over us, and the Queen Mother, herself breathing charm. This life of semi-friendship with Prime Ministers and members of the Royal Family will finish in six weeks' time and I shall have vanished from the scene as if I were dead, only if I were dead there would be a memorial service for me and *they* all would come.

Dinner at Claridge's with Elizabeth. She had spent two days with Rosamond Lehmann at Cumberland Lodge, Windsor Park (nicknamed Spook Hall), where there was a psychic convention. Elizabeth said there was much talk of reincarnation and that it gives one a pretty poor idea of God's resources to think that He could run out of inventing new people and be reduced to using the same old material over and over again. Elizabeth was in splendid form, but she is not cured. I fear for this winter when I am away in Canada.

John and Anne Maher are staying with us. We are a very companionable quartet. Anne seems to me as young in spirit as when I first knew her forty years ago, and I love her dearly.

September 27, 1971
We have left the house and are staying for a brief interlude at the Dorchester. Back last night on the night train from Scotland from staying with the Adeanes at Balmoral. Everything we do is now a last time—most certainly the last time I dine with the Queen at Balmoral.

October 25, 1971—Ottawa
The menacing wail of the vacuum cleaner wielded in the inept hands of our new cleaning woman comes nearer and nearer up the passage to my closed bedroom door, seeking what it can devour. The rain has peed itself out and on the still-wet streets the last leaves are falling. It is an autumn morning, still mild before the snow flies.

I am baffled by all this talk of the cultural opportunities of Ottawa, the Renaissance life one can lead at the Centre for the Performing Arts. I would rather walk the quiet back streets, beyond the cluster of high-rise apartments, down to the poorer quarters where a sort of sing-song, ding-dong life crawls along. The old sit on porches and stare. A little girl kicks up leaves in the gutter and chases a grey cat. China ornaments of no cultural significance encumber small windows choked with potted plants. Swarthy, big-bellied Italians park their dirty, dented old cars up wide alleys. Chinese children are playing football on an asphalt yard. On corner lots stand up the grey rock churches of the French-Canadian faith, flanked by priests' houses and seminaries, cheerless formal repositories, but preferred by me to the hulking red sandstone of the United Church, embodiment of gloomy, dowdy dullness.

At the cocktail party yesterday someone asked me point-blank across a roomful of people, "To what do you attribute your success as a diplomat?" I was somewhat taken aback by the question and was incapable, or unwilling, to make an answer, like ladies asked to account for the flavour of their curry soup. . . . "Oh, one just adds a snatch of pepper, a dash of salt and a few condiments."

All the same, the question has set me thinking, not so much of success or failure in the diplomatic career as of the profession of diplomacy, and specifically of the Canadian Foreign Service in which I have spent nearly forty years of my life and to which I am now saying goodbye.

*   *   *

Yet it was to be some time before I set down on paper the following reflections on diplomacy and diplomats— particularly the Canadian variety.

Diplomatic Attitudes

Diplomacy is a matter of communication. The first diplomats were no doubt the messengers sent from one cave to another to establish friendship or to issue defiance. Like ambassadors today, if the messages they bore were not agreeable to the recipients, they were apt to be unpopular (no doubt on the McLuhan principle that the medium is the message). Sometimes they were decapitated and their heads returned to the senders. Now they are declared persona non grata and are recalled by their own governments in a huff or as a prelude to hostilities. Yet sooner or later, after the war is over, the business of diplomacy is resumed and diplomatic channels are reopened. The process will continue indefinitely unless humanity succeeds in blowing itself off the earth's surface.

It is argued that the traditional methods of diplomacy and the system of representation abroad are out of date. Also, that the diplomats themselves are, in training and outlook, out of touch with the realities of today's world.

It is certainly true that the role of the diplomat has changed and is changing, and that diplomacy is being conducted in new spheres and by new methods. It would indeed be very extraordinary if, when every social and political institution is changing so rapidly, the diplomatic career remained as a sort of fossil of the past; if it did so, what young man of ability and ambition would wish to enter such a profession?

Much of this material appeared in *Spectrum* (Volume 3, Number 2, 1983), a quarterly publication of the Canadian Imperial Bank of Commerce, under the title "As Others See Us—Canada's Image Abroad".

Difficult, sometimes painful, problems of adjustment, together with new challenges, face the diplomat of today. His position is a vulnerable one. He is a generalist surrounded by experts. In a period when quantifiable coefficients are the instruments for assessing job performance, how does one measure such qualities as skill in negotiation, coolness in crisis, and experience in international affairs? And how does the diplomat fare in the company of specialists in a technological age? International negotiations cover so many fields undreamed of in the past, whether it be the environment, tariffs, energy, the law of the sea, the protection of human rights, monetary policy, or sport, that one can hardly think of an area of human activity which is not on the agenda of an international gathering.

Linked with this proliferation of new areas of negotiation has been the development of multilateral diplomacy, where negotiations are not just between two nations but among many. The United Nations is of course the most obvious case, but there are now more than 150 international organizations. Multilateral diplomacy, with its lobbying for support, its dealings with international secretariats, the variety of its subject matter, is a new phenomenon requiring both political skills and expert knowledge.

It is a strange paradox that while traditional diplomacy is under fire from so many quarters, diplomacy is one of the growth industries of this century. When I returned to Canada House in London in 1967, the number of foreign diplomats and their wives there entitled to varying degrees of diplomatic privileges and immunity totalled more than 3,300— more than double the number when I had last been stationed in London in 1945. All foreign service offices, like all other branches of bureaucracy, have increased vastly in size. New nations, between sixty and seventy of them since the last war, have come into being and have sent their new diplomats all around the world. In return, older nations have posted their diplomats to the new states.

Serving Canada abroad is an enlightening experience. The Canadian identity emerges very clearly when seen from the outside and when Canada appears as an actor on the international stage. Any foreign diplomat who has had the experience of negotiating with Canadians would recognize on sight our particular Canadian mix of goodwill and hard-headedness, of friendliness and touchiness. He would also, I think, respect the Canadian instinct for conciliation and realistic acceptance of the limits of the possible, mingled though it is with a strong dose of self-righteousness. These qualities do not seem to be more Anglo-Canadian than French-Canadian. Indeed, seen from abroad, all Canadians, whatever their differences of origin, seem much more like each other than like any other race or nation, including the races from which they spring.

In the longer perspective there also emerges a continuity in Canadian attitudes in international affairs. Despite changes of governments and varying emphasis in our foreign policies, it would be almost possible to foretell a Canadian national reaction to an international problem or crisis. The very vocabulary in which Canadian views are expressed has not much altered. It has a moralistic preaching tone which strives, sometimes inadequately, to express a real strain of idealism. Yet this idealism is inevitably strongly diluted by the realism of a great trading nation with the material interests of its people to safeguard. Any policy which drifted away too far from our national interests into an atmosphere of ideal international aspirations would have no roots at home.

When I entered it in 1934, the Department of External Affairs was as small as Canada's place then was on the map of international politics. Since then, of course, it has increased enormously in size and in complexity of organization. At the start we were anxious to differentiate ourselves from traditional Foreign Offices, to eschew diplomatic trappings and to display an almost-ostentatious lack of ostentation. The profession of diplomacy is, however, an international trade union which, whatever the national or individual styles and origins of its members, stamps them all with its hallmark. The Canadian diplomat, like all other diplomats, lives a peculiar amphibious existence at home and abroad. Abroad, one enjoys privileges, allowances, and a special status. At home, one is a civil servant among tens of thousands of others, and the quicker one adjusts to the change the better.

For the foreign service officer who is interested in policy and the mechanics of power, service at home is more important than service abroad. If he hopes to exert any influence on affairs he must make good his position in the department. The longer he remains abroad, remote from the political and departmental infighting in Ottawa, the more his influence tends to decline. He must first have established a base of trust and friendship at home in order to count on continued support, and this relationship must be steadily maintained. He who forgets this does so at his peril.

Power is at the centre, as Winston Churchill once remarked. It is in Ottawa that all the decisions are made that affect our policy abroad. Much has been written lately in Canada, as well as elsewhere, about the decision-making process in foreign policy, and much of it has been written by political scientists whose journals explore the subject, sometimes with the aid of graphs or models of behaviour. These methods have produced studies of value, although often couched in language so specialized that those actually involved in the decision-making—the politicians and officials—might find it hard to follow them without taking a language course. Such studies are conducted in a cool climate of reasoned analysis which is remote indeed from the pressure-cooker of politics.

In reality, decisions are often taken in reaction to unexpected developments in the international field—a sudden revolution, a change in interest rates abroad. At home there are pressures from other government departments with their special interests and responsibilities, and there are waves of public concern and agitation about particular causes. Sometimes policy swerves from its course from the urgent necessity of the government's winning a by-election, or because of a rash reply given by a Minister to an awkward question in the House of Commons. Then there are the time and human elements. As to the time element, in an age of instantaneous communications it is speeded up to a matter of moments in which a decision may have to be reached or a previous decision reversed. A telephone call from one national leader to another may do the trick. The human element involves not only the personalities of our politicians and their advisers but the effects of strain, fatigue, or ill-health.

Diplomats, when serving abroad, live in a different world, a world of official immunity. They are outside the law of the country where they are stationed. Diplomatic immunity is far from being an artificial anachronism. Without it, diplomats stationed in hostile countries could easily become the victims of trumped-up charges. Diplomatic immunity is often misunderstood and causes irritation to the local inhabitants. The aspect which causes most irritation is the diplomat's ability to park his car wherever he likes. In recent years the number of parking tickets issued to diplomats in one capital—London—and left unpaid numbered, over a ten-month period, more than twenty-six thousand. I am glad to say that, although not in law bound to do so, the personnel of Canadian missions abroad are under instruction to pay such fines.

There is no aspect of diplomatic life which appears to the outsider more artificial, and indeed sometimes more absurd, than that of protocol. There is a type of diplomat to whom matters of protocol come to assume absorbing fascination; there are others who regard them as a necessary evil. Protocol is best understood as a reflection of the extraordinary sensitivity and touchiness of the nation state. Nations, in their relations with each other, of which diplomats are simply the agents, behave very much like temperamental prima donnas. They fear "losing face" or being upstaged. They use the nuances of a snub or the extra cordiality of a gesture as a means of registering the temperature of their relations with other states. At what level of representation is a visiting Canadian Foreign Minister welcomed at the airport on arrival in a foreign country? How many guns are fired in salute for the arrival of a visiting Head of State? What is the degree of warmth or coolness expressed in an after-dinner toast? These apparently trivial things form a sort of code, carefully weighed and noted in the diplomatic community. They may be the first indications, the red or green light, in relations between states indicating degrees of friendship or hostility.

One of the features that separate diplomats in the higher ranks from others in the communities in which they live is their housing. This has always been a sensitive question for Canadians. Some critics would like the style of life of Canadian representatives abroad to reflect that of the average Canadian middle-class home. In practice, in most countries, ambassadors are housed in conditions quite different from anything that could be afforded by the local inhabitants. This dates back to the days when there were plenty of large private houses staffed by many servants, and the ambassador's residence was one of many, instead of standing out as an exception. One justification for maintaining these mansions is the necessity for entertaining. How much is diplomatic entertaining justified? Sometimes its value is greatly exaggerated, yet it still goes on all over the world. The Embassy provides a setting for hospitality to visitors from home and the local colony of Canadian residents, for entertaining politicians and officials in the country to which one is accredited and visiting Canadian Ministers. All this requires a certain scale of physical "plant".

Perhaps finally this whole way of life will disappear for one very simple reason—there will no longer be servants available—and ambassadors will have to retreat to modest flats and mount their dinners and receptions at the local hotels. They will then be faced by the great and growing problem of physical security. When I was in Washington, the Prime Minister, Mike Pearson, came on a visit and we gave a dinner for him and the President, L. B. Johnson, and their wives. This involved the presence in the Embassy residence and grounds of some twenty United States security men. The cook threatened to leave. "They kept tracking through my kitchen," she complained, "while I am trying to cook the dinner." She also resented having to prepare a light repast for the security officers simultaneously with the dinner upstairs.

Women diplomats in the higher ranks are still something of a rarity in all Foreign Services. In our own Foreign Service we have had a handful of distinguished women diplomats—too few and too far between. The unsung heroines of the Foreign Service are the women in its administrative and secretarial ranks, without whom the whole operation would speedily collapse. The attractions for Canadians of representing their country abroad are less than they once were. With the opening up of missions in so many new countries, the ratio of unhealthy, remote, and boring posts has increased. Then, too, some wives of foreign service officers—and this is increasingly the case—have interesting, remunerative jobs at home and do not look forward to the prospect of giving them up in order to accompany their husbands to a foreign post. Yet the wife of a foreign service officer can make all the difference to the success or failure of her husband's posting abroad. If she enjoys the stimulus of meeting a variety of people, if she finds an interest in getting to know other countries and cultures, the husband and wife

make a doubly effective team. I do not know how effective
Sylvia and I have been as a team—I do know that without her
I could not have carried on. She has risen to every occasion
with zest and without fuss.

By its very nature this is a career of adjustments not only
to changes of place but to changes of policy and changes of
political masters. This involves conformity, but when does
the conformity stop? What happens in the process to the
personal convictions of the individual?

It is sometimes suggested that diplomats have suspi-
ciously supple consciences, and accommodate themselves all
too easily to changing régimes and switches in policy; that
they serve not only their country "right or wrong" but any
government in power "right or wrong". There is a lot of
truth in the saying that "there are old diplomats and bold
diplomats, but there are no old bold diplomats." It is not a
profession for men of fiery political opinions. They should go
into politics and fire them off there—but that does not
necessarily mean that all diplomats are a race of spineless
time-servers without views of their own. Certainly there has
been no lack of debate and dissension over policy in the ranks
of our own foreign service. Most of the important—and some
of the unimportant—decisions in our foreign policy have been
the subject of discussion in which professional diplomats
played an active part, sometimes seeing their views prevail,
sometimes being overruled by the Foreign Minister or the
Prime Minister. If overruled, these same officials proceeded
to defend abroad the policies which at home they had tried to
alter. This for some was a painful duty, but they had no
doubt that it was their duty. If that is what is meant by
conformist, a good diplomat is a good conformist. Once a
line of policy is adopted, and it is a matter of explaining it and
defending it abroad, there is no longer any place for personal
differences. It is the diplomat's role to convey as accurately
and as cogently as possible the policy of his government. If he

aired his own views to a foreign government or to the press, he would be misleading them. However much he protested that his view was personal, it would be believed that it reflected in some measure the views of his government. An ambassador or a senior official in a Foreign Office is only worth while listening to if his interlocutor believes that he is in close touch with the opinion of his own government and has authority to express it. The ambassador's personal opinions are of no more importance to a foreign government than those of a taxi driver, and often less interesting.

Of course, there are outer limits to loyalty, and if one believes that the policies of one's government are evil or dangerous to the interests of one's country, one has always the recourse of resignation. It must be admitted that on the whole, diplomats do not resign readily. They sometimes console themselves with the reflection that if they left the service, a more dangerous and undesirable person might be appointed in their place.

A diplomat is a civil servant at the orders of his government who happens to be serving part of his life abroad. Under the orders of his government, yes, but under how many and how different governments in the course of a lifetime? As for myself, I have served under six Prime Ministers in the course of my career—a mixed bunch, one might irreverently remark. Some I have known better than others; most I have observed at pretty close quarters at home and abroad.

The only people to whom Prime Ministers can talk on a basis of real equality are other Prime Ministers. I have been present at many such "face-to-face" meetings between Canadian Prime Ministers and their counterparts in foreign countries. In addition to the importance of the official agenda for discussion between them, it was fascinating to watch the manner in which they took each other's measure. There was always a period of small talk between the great men, customarily led off by a few mild jokes. Nothing of significance at this stage was said by either party, but if they were meeting for the first time they seemed to sense, not only on political grounds but on grounds of sympathy or aversion, whether this relationship would bear fruit in future. This matter of personal rapport or distaste between the leaders of nations is one of those elements in international affairs least easy to forecast, escaping all computerized data and baffling the planners, but by no means negligible in its effects. Two examples are the personal antipathy between President Kennedy and Prime Minister Diefenbaker, and the personal friendship between Mr. St. Laurent and Mr. Nehru. It is not always the antagonist in the international arena who arouses personal mistrust—it is sometimes the ally.

In the conduct of Canadian foreign policy the effects of prime-ministerial or ministerial statements on international issues which are aimed at vote-getting at home, without regard for the long-term consequences abroad, are much to be feared. However, what really counts in the daily conduct of foreign policy is that the Secretary of State for External Affairs should have a strong position in Cabinet and be able to make his views prevail. A Foreign Minister may be a charming chap, much liked by his officials, but that is of little use if the policies he is advocating are regularly shot down by his colleagues or overruled by the Prime Minister. Of course, in the worst case one may have a Minister who is both disagreeable and ineffectual.

It is notoriously difficult to get Canadian news into the columns of the foreign press. As I know all too well, it is easier for the camel to enter the eye of the needle than to get a well-informed Canadian political story or considered editorial comment into the columns of the press of London, Paris, or New York. Perhaps this is in part simply because our news stories are not very sensational; perhaps if we indulged in more revolutions, or more spectacular scandals or crimes, we would receive more attention. There are far too few Canadian journalists permanently stationed abroad and too many journalists accompanying visiting Canadian ministers. Our actors, singers, and artists contribute enormously to a fuller view of Canada.

Politicians of all stripes are very prone to tell us what a great people we are and what a magnificent future awaits us if we vote the right way, or, alternatively, to chide us for backsliding if we do not fulfil their expectations by conforming to their policies. Fortunately, Canadians have enough common sense not to swallow all these congratulations and admonitions. Canadian governments have always had a tendency to dish out good advice to other nations, calling upon them to behave themselves in conformity with our high moral standards, and to cease and desist from disturbing actions. We are a little too apt to insist by contrast upon the purity of our own intentions. We have the more cause to be careful of the susceptibilities of other peoples because we are extremely susceptible to criticism of ourselves by others. This prickly sensitivity is not an asset to us.

We show to our best advantage in our association with the developing nations. We ourselves have gone through a colonial stage in our history and know something of the birth pangs of emerging nationhood. Our relationship with such countries also brings to the surface the idealist strain that has always played a part both in our aid programs and in our peace-keeping initiatives. In general, we are happier when we can fulfil a practical and humanitarian or peace-keeping role, and this has brought us many good friends around the world. We resent condescension, real or imagined. "Who the hell do they think they are?" is the common Canadian reaction. Sometimes this attitude comes into play even in our relations with those with whom we have the closest ties of friendship and affinity—the British, the French, and the Americans. We condemn in others what seems to us snobbery, cultural or social, whereas while we have no class structure in the

European or even the American sense, we have many social and cultural dividing lines of our own, and quite a plentiful crop of snobs.

It is a well-worn platitude that in a democracy foreign policy should be based upon an alert and informed public opinion, but to repeat a truism does not make it come true. The fact is that most people, most of the time, are not much interested in foreign policy except when it touches their pockets or involves some special group organized for a particular cause. This lack of interest is reflected in this country in the paucity of public debate in and out of Parliament and the scrappy coverage (with some honourable exceptions) of international affairs in the press. Thus, informed public opinion is, and is likely to remain, in a minority.

It is, however, a minority essential to the conduct of foreign affairs, for a policy which has no real roots in public opinion is apt to be an artificial construction which may sound plausible on paper, but which collapses at any real test. The universities and the press have, of course, an indispensable part to play, informing and sustaining public interest. In Canada we have been fortunate in having an academic community who are making valuable contributions to our knowledge and understanding of foreign policy issues.

Those who operate in the field of international relations, politicians and professional diplomats, depend upon such informed comment. Even criticism is preferable to indifference; otherwise they may come to feel that they are functioning in a void, and no one likes to feel superfluous, not even an ambassador—or, indeed, an old ex-ambassador.

As to the vexed question of our national identity, it appears that, in the long run, despite all our self-doubts and divisions, we have an instinctive sense of what it means to be Canadian and no intention of relinquishing the privilege. Sometimes this seems clearer viewed from a distant perspective than closer at home.

Epilogue

As it turned out, my farewell to diplomacy did not lead to a farewell to the Public Service of Canada. For on December 9, 1971, I was appointed Special Advisor to the Privy Council in Ottawa. My diary entry for that day reads as follows: "They have announced my appointment to the Privy Council. The front-page headline of the *Ottawa Journal* says 'Government Crumbles' and, directly below, 'Ritchie Joins the Prime Minister's Office'. It sounds as though I had been called in to prop up the edifice. In reality this job has nothing to do with party politics. What precisely it *has* to do with remains to be seen. At any rate it gives me one more hand to play before I throw in the cards and clear out for good. Then I shall delve once more into the toppling piles of my diaries to see if anything can be unearthed that will bear the light of day."

Index

Abu Dhabi, Sheik of, 133
Acheson, Alice, 25, 40, 74
Acheson, Dean, 5, 25, 40, 74, 75, 83, 84
Adeane, Michael, 91, 152
Africa, 109-10
Afternoon Men, 117
Ailleret, Gen. and Mme, 101
Allport, Lady, 95
Almon, Eliza, 7
Alphand, Hervé, 86
Alsop, Joseph, 10
Alsop, Susan Mary, 10, 29
Amory, Derick, 131
Ancient, Miss ("Anan"), 56-7
Anderson, William, 97-8
Annandale (Georgia), 45
Anne, Princess, 148
Anne-Marie, Princess Callimachi, 66
Anti-Memoirs, 102-3
Antony and Cleopatra, 126
Armstrong, William, 52
Asquith, Lady Cynthia, 105-6
Astor, Lady Nancy, 117-18

Bacon, Virginia, 68
Balásy, Tony, 26-7
Ball, George, 14, 42, 74, 75

Barco, Jim, 13
Beale, Sir Howard and Lady, 64
Beaufort, Duke and Duchess of, 103
Benson, Edgar, 117
Berlin, Isaiah, 74
Bessborough, Earl and Countess of, 107, 126
Best, Dr. Charles, 148
Bliss, Mrs. Robert Woods, 68
Boland, Freddy, 11
Boston, 58, 70
Bowen, Elizabeth, 102, 108, 130, 134, 143; visit to Washington, 25; recalls Bloomsbury world, 94; author's visits to Hythe, 105, 115, 124-5, 142; reviews of *Eva Trout,* 120, 125; loyalty, 133; visit to Bowen's Court, 146; on reincarnation, 151
Brandon, Henry, 9, 12, 17, 37
Breese, William and Nora, 38
Brooke, Rupert, 126
Brown, George, 91
Brussels, 86
Buchan, Alastair, 39
Buchan, John, Baron Tweedsmuir, 39

Budget (1963), 52, 60
Bundy, McGeorge, 3, 32, 36, 74-5, 81, 82, 83, 84
Bundy, William and Mary, 25, 40, 73
Butterworth, Walter, 76
Byron, Lord, 27, 50, 51

Cadieux, Marcel, 114
Callaghan, Morley, 42
Camp David, 80-1
Campbell, Ross, 31
Canada: role in U.K. and U.S. relations, 5; Cuban policy, 16-17; dealings with Communist countries, 17; nuclear weapons, 16, 22-3, 32, 52; Cuban missile crisis, 23-4; viewed from abroad, 30-1, 156; anti-Americanism, 34; election campaign (1963), 46; survival as independent state, 50; Budget (1963), 52, 60; French military forces withdraw from NATO, 85-6; changes in role in NATO, 104-5; Trudeau's government, 136-8; kidnappings (1970), 145; Canadian identity, 156, 165; attitudes in international affairs, 156; decision-making in foreign policy, 157-8; daily conduct of foreign policy, 163; news in foreign press, 163-4; attitudes in dealing with other nations, 164; foreign policy, 165. *See also* Canada–U.K.

relations; Canada–U.S. relations
Canada at Britain's Side, 89, 90
Canada–U.K. relations: in days of Vincent Massey, 89-90; African nations in Commonwealth, 109-10, 119; anti-NATO feeling in Canada, 114; position in 1969, 129
Canada–U.S. relations: strained between Diefenbaker and Kennedy governments, 1-3, 5, 13, 50; meeting between Pearson and Kennedy, 48-9; Budget (1963), 52, 60; author's view, 53; contacts in Washington affecting, 71; Vietnam War, 77; Pearson's speech, 80; Pearson's meeting with Johnson, 80-2
Carpaccio, 43
Carscallen, Mary, 116
Chester (N.S.), 110-11, 112
Chevrier, Lionel, 86
China, 17
Christian, Lady Hesketh ("Kisty"), 102, 149
civil rights, 60
Civilisation, 141
Clark, Kenneth, 141
Cobbold, Lord and Lady, 130
Colin (butler), 15-16, 39, 46, 47, 52, 65
Commonwealth, 12, 90, 91, 109, 110
communism, 53
Companion of Canada, 129, 133-4

Cooper, Lady Diana, 35, 38, 133, 141-2
Coster, William, 144
Cross, Jasper, 145n., 146
Cuba, 16-17
Cuban missile crisis (1962), 23
Czech crisis (1968), 112

Dallas, 29, 30
Darwall, Lale, 105
Death of the Heart, The, 142
Defence of Poetry, A, 50
de Gaulle, Gen. Charles, 64, 85, 86, 104
Department of External Affairs: author's reminiscences, 19-20; attitude, 37; after Pearson's election, 61; family life of diplomat, 63; Embassy staff, 71; accommodation, 112; author's view of function, 114; new economies, 135; under Trudeau, 138; emphasis in 1934, 156-7
Devon, 131
Devonshire, Andrew, 133
Diefenbaker, John G.: author's appointment to Washington, 1; Kennedy's attitude, 2, 3, 6, 163; Cuban missile crisis, 23, 24; nuclear weapons, 24; U.S. interference in Canadian affairs, 32, 33; government defeated, 32-3; election campaign (1963), 34, 37-8; defeated, 47, 48; role in Canada–U.S. relations, 50

diplomats: changing role, 154-5; service at home and abroad, 157; immunity, 158; protocol, 158-9; ambassador's residence, 159; security officers, 160; women, 160; wives, 160-1; temperament, 161; role, 161-2; civil servant, 162; conversations between Prime Ministers, 162-3
Dobrynin, Anatoly, 13, 36
Dobrynin, Mme, 13
Don Juan, 27
Dulles, Allan and Clover, 69
Dulles, John Foster, 69
Dumbarton Oaks, 9
Durrell, Lawrence, 11

Elizabeth II, 103, 152
Elizabeth, Queen Mother, 151
Elliston, Peter, 100-1, 120
European Common Market, 4, 34
Eva Trout, 94, 120, 125
Evening Standard (London), 87

Farquharson, Robert, 63
Feaver, Temp, 20
Fleming, Ian and Anne, 133
France, 85-6, 104, 129
Fraser, Blair, 96
Freedman, Max, 4-5

Garwood (butler), 97-8, 101
Genet, Jean, 28
Germany, 36, 41, 49
Getty, Paul, 142
Geylins, Mr. and Mrs., 25
Gordon, Walter, 52n.

Green, Howard, 1, 22, 24, 33, 47
Greenhill, Dennis, 91, 145
Grünewald, Mathias, 21

Halifax, 17, 59-60
Halton, Matthew and Jean, 103-4
Ham House, 100
Hammarskjöld, Dag, 74
Hampshire, Stuart and Elizabeth, 133
Hardy, Jerry, 91, 99, 115, 129
Harkness, Douglas, 24
Harriman, Averell, 74, 84
Hartley, Leslie, 133
Heath, Edward, 95, 136, 146
Heeney, Arnold, 1, 8, 15
Hohenlohe, Princess, 46
Home, Alec, 91
Hood, Viscount Samuel, 67-8
House in Paris, The, 142
Howland, Dick, 15, 29
Hudd, Frederic, 101
Hutchison, Bruce, 40
Hyannisport (Mass.), 48
Hythe, 105, 115, 124, 134, 142-3

Ignatieff, George, 45n., 85
Ignatieff, Michael and Andrew, 45-6
Interest Equalization Tax, 72

Johnson, Lady Bird, 81
Johnson, Lyndon B., 70, 77-84, 160

Kaunda, Kenneth, 109
Kennedy, Caroline, 6
Kennedy, John F.: relations with Diefenbaker, 1, 2, 3, 6, 163; impressions of, 6, 64-5; view of professional diplomats, 9-10; friendship with Henry Brandon, 17; Cuban missile crisis, 23, 24; Nassau Agreement, 32; lunch with Diana Cooper, 35; meeting with Pearson, 48-9; visit to Europe, 52-3; relationship with diplomats, 61, 62, 75; assassination, 70; Pearson's tribute to, 79
Kennedy, Joseph P., 10
Kennedy, Robert, 49, 70, 106
Kent, Duchess of, 148, 149
kidnappings, 145
King, William Lyon Mackenzie, 67, 89, 113
Knebworth, 130

Lamb, Caroline, 51
Laporte, Pierre, 145
Lauderdale, Lord, 100
Léger, Jules, 64
Lehmann, Rosamond, 151
Leiter, Oatsie, 34
LePan, Douglas, 87, 148
Letters of Credence, 4, 6
Lippmann, Walter, 2, 9, 35, 79
Little Girls, The, 25
Loelia, Duchess of Westminster, 150
London, 87, 90, 93, 106, 158

Longworth, Alice, 64-5, 68
Loved and the Lost, The, 42

McCulley, Joseph, 54-5, 57
Macdonald, Mr. and Mrs.
   Donald, 132
McLaughlin, Earl, 122
Macmillan, Harold, 4, 32, 139
McMillan, J. R., 129
McNamara, Robert S., 26, 75
Maher, Anne, 151-2
Maher, John, 99, 151
Making of the President, 1960,
   The, 8
Mallett, Donald, 119
Malraux, André, 102-3
Manchester, 139-41
Marler, Sir Herbert, 71
Marshall, Young, 126
Marshall Plan, 53
Martin, Cynthia, 38
Martin, Paul, 65
Massey, Vincent, 21, 89
Matsas, Alexandros, 37, 60
Meagher, Margaret, 139
Mitford, Nancy, 147
Moore, Doris, 50
Morrison, Harold, 41
Morse, Sen. Wayne, 65
Mountolive, 11
Mrs. Dalloway, 93
Mulley, Mrs., 96
Murray, Geoff, 91

Nassau Agreement, 27, 32
NATO: Canada's value to U.S.,
   16; nuclear weapons on

Canadian soil, 24, 32; German
   role, 36; Dean Acheson on, 41;
   Pearson's speech, 83;
   withdrawal of French military
   forces, 85-6; Trudeau's view,
   90; Canada's changing role,
   104-5, 106, 114; Trudeau's
   meeting with Harold Wilson,
   123; commemorative service,
   130
Nehru, Jawaharlal, 163
New York, 10, 11, 21-2
New York Times, 9
Nicolson, Harold, 116
NORAD, 23
Norstad, Gen. Lauris, 24
North Atlantic Council, 85-6
nuclear weapons, 16, 22-3, 24,
   32, 52, 53
Nyerere, Julius, 109

O'Brien, Larry, 117
O'Brien, Scruff, 64
Odell, Misses, 18
Organization of American States,
   16
Ormsby-Gore, David, 73
Ottawa, 17, 33-4, 68, 112, 152
Ourousoff, Mr. and Mrs., 38
Oxford, 87, 134-5

Payne, Tony, 123
Paris, 85, 86
Pearson, Lester B. ("Mike"):
   Diefenbaker's suspicion, 2;
   election plans, 4; nuclear
   weapons, 24-5; becomes Prime

Minister, 47; relations with
Kennedy, 48-9, 80; author's
work in Washington, 61;
personality, 60, 72-3; Dean
Acheson on, 74, 83; relations
with U.S. Ambassador, 76;
relations with Lyndon Johnson,
79-84; speech on Vietnam
bombing, 80; author's
appointment to London, 86;
different style from Trudeau,
90; visit to London, 96-7;
Bobby Kennedy's assassination,
106; on NATO, 106;
relationship with Harold
Wilson, 124; kidnapping crisis
(1970), 145; security at
Embassy, 160
Pearson, Maryon, 4, 96, 106
Pendennis, 146
Pepin, Jean-Luc, 132
Perin, Anne, 38
Perron, Annette, 49
Philadelphia, 80
Philip, Prince, 10
Phillips, Mr. and Mrs., 35
Pickering College, 54-8
Pictures and Conversation, 125
Plymouth, 117-18
Powell, Anthony, 74, 117, 151
Prime Ministers, 162-3
protest marches, 99-100
protocol, 158-9

Quebec, 90, 126, 145

Rae, Bob, 139
Rasminsky, Louis, 72

Reston, James ("Scotty"), 9, 25-
6, 75, 79
Ritchie, Charles Stewart Almon:
appointed Ambassador to
Washington (1962), 1;
impression of Kennedy, 6; on
grandmother, 7; religion, 8,
21, 119, 149; Dumbarton
Oaks, 9; on New York, 10,
21-2; friendships in U.N., 11;
blandness of Washington, 11;
negative attitude of U.S.
toward Commonwealth, 12;
reminiscences of Department,
19-20; viewing Canada from
abroad, 30-1, 156; tour of
Texas, 29-30; U.S. press
release on Canadian
government, 32-3;
manufactured anti-
Americanism, 34; dreaming,
36; on niece, 37; position in
Washington, 38, 43, 61; on
Bruce Hutchison, 40; on the
English, 40; on Carpaccio's
work, 43; Loyalist roots, 45;
election (1963), 46, 47;
meeting between Pearson and
Kennedy, 48-9; Canada's
survival as independent state,
50; influence of the dead on
the living, 51; national
anthem, 51-2; U.S. policies on
international affairs, 53-4;
teaching at Pickering College,
54-8; as schoolboy, 55, 87;
mother's illness, 58-9; on Mike
Pearson, 60, 72-3; diplomatic

parties, 61; National Days, 62-3; diplomatic life for families, 63; on Paul Martin, 65; junior officers, 65-6; on Hume Wrong, 66-7; on Allan Dulles, 69; J. F. Kennedy's assassination, 70; telephone in diplomatic work, 72; duties in Washington, 70-2; relations with State Department, 73-4; on Dean Acheson, 74; dealings with White House, 74-5; journalists, 75; diplomatic colleagues, 75; friends in Washington, 76; diaries, 77, 115-16, 117, 118-19, 120, 122; Vietnam War, 77; on Lyndon Johnson, 77-84; at Camp David, 81-3; appointed to North Atlantic Council (1966), 85; on Paris, 85, 86; appointed High Commissioner to London (1966), 86-9; importance of London in author's life, 87; on Vincent Massey, 89; Canada–U.K. relations, 89; dealings with U.K. government, 91; staff at Canada House, 91; functions of High Commissioner, 92; on making his mark, 93; politicians, 96; Pearson's visit to London, 96-7; comments on world situation (1968), 99-100; protest marches, 100, 120; visit to Ham House, 100; visits the Sitwells, 101-2, 149; impressions of Trudeau, 102,

113-14, 136-8; Canada's role in NATO, 104-5, 106; visits with Elizabeth Bowen at Hythe, 105, 115, 124-5, 142; visit to Stansted, 107-8, 126; Canada's position in Commonwealth, 109-10; holiday in Chester (N.S.), 110-11, 112; on "being offended", 111; Czech crisis (1968), 111-12; official visit to Plymouth, 117-18; on Arnold Smith, 119; Lord Mayor's dinner, 121; pleasures in life, 122-23; Trudeau's meeting with Harold Wilson, 123-4; on great-great aunt, 125; Trudeau's plan for greater participation in government, 127; changes in lifestyle of diplomats, 127-8; Companion of Canada, 129, 133-4; at Knebworth, 130; on Derick Amory, 131; on Jean-Luc Pepin, 132; duties in London, 136; visit to Manchester, 139-41; escapes from habitual behaviour, 141; kidnapping crisis (1970), 145; on Ted Heath, 146; on Harold Wilson, 146; the younger generation, 147; on Nancy Mitford, 147; retirement, 148, 151, 169; on Anthony Powell, 151; changing methods of diplomacy, 154-5; Canadian identity, 156, 165; service at home and abroad, 157;

decision-making in foreign
policy, 157-8; diplomatic
immunity, 158; protocol, 158-
9; ambassador's residence, 159;
security officers, 160; women
diplomats, 160; wives of
diplomats, 160-1;
temperament of diplomat,
161; role of diplomat, 161;
civil servant, 162;
conversations between Prime
Ministers, 162-3; daily conduct
of foreign policy, 163;
Canadian news in foreign press,
163-4; Canada's attitude in
dealing with other nations,
164; Canada's foreign policy,
165; appointed Special Advisor
to Privy Council (1971), 166
Ritchie, Ed, 145, 148
Ritchie, Elizabeth (niece), 18, 37,
120, 121, 126, 128
Ritchie, Lilian (mother), 18, 19,
51, 58, 129, 150
Ritchie, Roland (brother) and
Bunny, 17, 18, 110
Ritchie, Sylvia (wife), 2, 8, 15,
18, 27, 28, 35, 39, 43, 44,
46, 51, 60, 70, 76, 88, 95-6,
100, 101, 104, 106, 107,
115, 116, 117, 119, 125,
139, 140, 148, 161
Rive, Alfred, 20
Robertson, Norman, 22, 61, 123,
144
Robinson, Basil, 31, 71
Rogers, June, 92
Rogers, Louis, 91, 92, 135, 136,
149

Roosevelt, Theodore, 64
Rostow, Walter, 84
Rowan, John, 88
Rowley, Roger, 116, 120
Rusk, Dean, 2, 3, 19, 41, 73, 75
Ryan, Nin, 37

St. Laurent, Louis, 49, 163
Saul, William and Beryl, 98
separatism, 129
Sharp, Mitchell, 14, 114
Sharpe, John, 63
Shelley, Percy Bysshe, 50
Shenstone, Michael, 65
Sinclair, Huntley, 103
Sitwell, Sacheverell and Georgia,
101-2, 149
Smith, Arnold, 91, 109, 119
Smith, Matthew, 125
Stansted, 107-8, 126
Stephens, Llyn, 54
Stewart, Harry, 16
Stoker, Chairman of Manchester
Liners, 140
Stone, Thomas and Alix, 44
Strachey, Lytton, 94, 96
student riots, 99-100
Sunday Times, 12
Swiggum, Comdr., 107

Tennant, Stephen, 99
Texas, 29-30
Thackeray, William Makepeace,
18, 146
Thomson, Roy, 136
Tolstoy, 119
Trend, Sir Burke, 139
Tristan, 150
Trudeau, Pierre E.: becomes

Prime Minister, 90, 103;
impressions, 102, 113-14,
136-8; Commonwealth
Conference (1968), 109;
"Establishment's" uneasiness,
113; meeting with Harold
Wilson, 123-4; reception at
Canada House, 125; aims for
greater participation in
government, 127;
dehumanization of life and
environment, 139, 140
Tyler, William, 52

Ulysses (Tennyson), 55
Union of Soviet Socialist
Republics: Harold Macmillan
on, 4; Soviet Ambassador, 13,
36; Cuban missile crisis, 23;
John Watkins on, 41-2;
nuclear weapons, 53; Czech
crisis, 112
United Kingdom: relations with
U.S., 5; Dean Acheson on, 40;
developments during 1966-71,
92-3, 99; Polish Ambassador
on recovery, 99; relations with
Africa, 109. *See also* Canada–
U.K. relations
United Nations, 11, 30
United States: relations with
U.K., 5; attitude on
Commonwealth, 12; outlook
in international affairs, 16, 53-
4; dealing with Communist
countries, 17; nuclear weapons,
23, 53; Cuban missile crisis,
23-4; press release on Canadian
government, 32; Budget
(1963), 52, 60; importance of
ambassadorial rank, 62;
Interest Equalization Tax, 72;
State Department, 73-4;
Lyndon Johnson, 77-83; NATO
allies, 83; demonstration at
Embassy in London, 120. *See
also* Canada–U.S. relations
Ustinov, Peter, 108

Valenti, Jack, 81, 83
Vanity Fair, 18
Vietnam War, 77, 80, 81

Wagner, 150
Walpole, Horace, 100
Washington: spring, 3-4, 5-6;
blandness, 11; "In" and
"Out" people, 17; summer,
51; civil-rights parade, 60;
social life, 67-9; journalists, 75;
friendships, 76
Watkins, John, 41-2
Weston Hall, 101-2
Wheeler-Bennett, John, 44
White, T. H., 8
Whitlock, W. C., 125-6
Wilson, Harold, 91, 99, 110,
121, 123-4, 146
Winkler, M. and Mme, 25
Woolf, Virginia, 93-4
Wrong, Hume, 5, 62, 66, 67, 92